# Stage 4

# Stage 4

*Surviving Cancer &*

*the Grief That*

*Comes*

*With*

*It*

# EMILY STERNS

ARCHWAY
PUBLISHING

Archway Publishing books may be ordered through booksellers or by contacting:

Archway Publishing
1663 Liberty Drive
Bloomington, IN 47403
www.archwaypublishing.com
844-669-3957

ISBN: 978-1-6657-4936-7 (sc)
ISBN: 978-1-6657-4935-0 (hc)
ISBN: 978-1-6657-4937-4 (e)

Library of Congress Control Number: 2023916319

Print information available on the last page.

Archway Publishing rev. date: 10/27/2023

# Contents

**Part 4: 2023**

# Introduction

Grief, a five-letter word that has been said to have five distinct stages. First comes denial, then anger, followed by bargaining, depression, and lastly, acceptance. It should be a simple path to follow, moving from one stage to the next. That couldn't be further from the truth. Grief is an all-consuming emotion that ebbs and flows throughout our lives, and there's no one right or wrong way to go through it. Yet the one element of grief that we all experience is survivorship. Grief happens because someone has left us, and we must move on and live life without that person. But how does one do that when you've lost yourself? There are times in our lives where we'll have an experience that will change us forever, and often we don't come out unscathed.

In general, grief is something that's universally understood, but each individual person experiences and goes through grief differently. There's no right way to grieve, no right time or length. Despite this, there's constant criticism surrounding how people grieve. Grieving won't look the same from person to person—there's no cookie-cutter mold, yet we somehow expect others to have the same reaction as us.

This is a story about grief. My grief. The grief I felt as I lost myself in my battle with stage 4 cancer. It was a process that undeniably shattered my life, the path I was on, and who I was to my core. I can't go back in time to be who I was before this journey started, but I can share what I went through as I discovered who I now am and will become.

PART ONE

# What Is Grief?

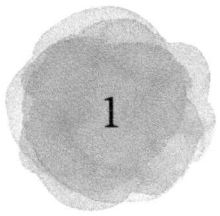

# I Thought I Knew Grief

Prior to my understanding that I was in a period of grief while battling cancer, I thought I knew what grief was—an immense sadness that covers every part of your life until it seems like you're consumed by it and then must fight your way through it to make it to the other side. The other side being some miraculous transformation into a new person, often a better person than you were before. Without thinking about it, year by year, we change as people based upon what has happened to us and around us. I never wanted to go through a transformation in this way. I didn't want to become a new and better person because I got sick and had to battle not only the disease but also the grief in losing myself through this life-altering event.

I'd been in the trenches of grief before. I was anxious, depressed, and ready to end it all in my teenage years. I shed tears, ate to fill the void, attempted to sleep away the pain, and even drank away the pain to feel only temporary relief. I've experienced life-altering events throughout my life. Beginning in my early childhood into my adolescence, death had come knocking on the doors of my family. I lost friends as I entered my early twenties and had breakups that shattered the world around me. Grief has always seemed to find its way back to me in every stage of my life.

When I was younger, I didn't have the tools at my disposal to help, and even if I had, I'm not sure I'd have used them in the same way. Part of me knows I used the not-so-healthy coping mechanisms in my later teens and early twenties to avoid the pain on the outside, but deep down, I felt it and would get lost in it because I was desperate to feel something. I was stuck in a cycle of wanting to feel better but not knowing how to fully get there. I'd find fleeting moments of happiness and cling to them before the next tidal wave of pain would crash over me.

I went to my first wake and funeral at the age of eight in 2005. I remember being devastated about not only this loss but also the two subsequent losses occurring in September 2006 and March 2007. Over this period, I lost my dad's best friend, my uncle Barry, my paternal grandfather (Grandpa Jim), and my mom's best friend, whom I called ZeeZeeZella. They were a huge part of my life growing up, and they all died rather quickly. My parents weren't set up to cope with the trauma this caused them, let alone help my older sister and me through this time. When I was told my uncle Barry was dead, I was in utter shock. I'd seen him the day before. No one thought that he would get in his car to drive home and it would be the last time we saw him.

On the other hand, I witnessed my grandpa Jim and ZeeZeeZella wither away rather quickly. It took years for the trauma of these deaths to really take center stage and for the effects to be visible on the outside. Internally, I was extremely mad that these people integral to my life had been taken from me, yet I lacked the ability to put those feelings into words. I transformed from a carefree child to one who understood the fragility of life too young. Eventually, these feelings manifested themselves outwardly by the time I was fourteen years old, and I began therapy for the first time.

Despite this, nothing prepared me for the grief I was experiencing as I began to slowly lose myself battling cancer while on the verge of becoming healthy again. When the realization hit that I was in a state of deep grief, I went online to find someone who could relate. I wanted to find a book that would help, I wanted to know someone else out there felt the way I did, and I craved the privacy of reading about it rather than talking about it. As an avid reader who has spent periods of time clutching onto pages of a book whose words have held me together more than people have, I knew there had to be someone else in the world who would know what I was feeling and had written about it.

I didn't want to read about someone else's cancer journey and how it all worked out for them—that wasn't what I wanted to hear. I was in the belly of the beast feeling angry and lost; I wanted someone who felt like that and could talk me off the ledge because they had been there too. I wanted someone to shed the true reality I was facing without covering it up in sunshine, saying it all worked out in the end. Sure, this may sound cynical, but that's how I felt, and I wanted my feelings to be validated. This led me to google the best books about grief, and a slew of titles popped up.

I scrolled down to a website listing the twenty-six best books on grief for 2022. Most of the books on the list had titles specific to grief relating to the death of someone—those books didn't appeal to me this time because no one had died. I was very much alive, just missing a huge chunk of who I was. Yet I found Megan Devine's book *It's OK That You're Not OK: Meeting Grief and Loss in a Culture That Doesn't Understand.*

After reading the synopsis of the book, I immediately went to my local Barnes & Noble and bought it. It sat on my nightstand for months before I had the courage to open it. I had this feeling that the words inside this book could have the power to make everything I was feeling make sense, and in a way, that was scary. I knew I was grieving and needed to work through it to continue living my life in an upward curve instead of a downward spiral. It took a while to be able to come to terms with all I had gone through the past few months. It took some time, but eventually, I felt mentally strong enough to read it and put in the work to really heal—to say it changed my life doesn't do it justice. I chose this book because the title mentioned how our culture in the United States doesn't understand grief and loss on an individual level and I needed it to.

Without even opening the book, I saw that the author, Megan, had lost her partner, Matt, to a freak accident. Meanwhile, I was diagnosed with stage 4 cancer at the age of twenty-six. On the outside, it might seem like our grief would have nothing in common, but that's where you're wrong. Grief is universal, and the foundation of it is the same—something has been taken from us in an unjust way. Furthermore, Megan looks at the Unites States as a whole and takes a psychological and sociological approach to understanding the inability we have as a society to be there for one another during the darkest periods in our lives. Her message is that only when you understand that you will never understand what someone else is going through can you offer support that helps. This is the mantra that got me through.

# 2

# The Culture Surrounding Grief

In the introduction to Megan Devine's book *It's OK That You're Not OK,* she discusses how in our culture we see grief as an emotional period that needs to be cleaned up and sorted as soon as possible.[1] The society in which we live sees grief as short-lived and unnecessary to dwell in rather than something that can be tended to. When we are slow to overcome grief or are seen tending it, we are then often criticized, critiqued, and shamed for how we have chosen to behave in this deeply emotional and personal state.

I remember feeling embarrassed to tell my closest friends or family that I was struggling. When I entered remission and then got the courage to talk to someone about how I felt like I had lost myself and didn't know who I was anymore, I got brushed off. It was assumed, since I was considered healthy again, that my life would go back to normal. I was questioned how I could be struggling with who I was as a person because they thought I was the same as I'd always been. That couldn't have been further from the truth. I wanted to yell through my texts to make them understand that I could never be the same after what I had gone through, and no matter how much they wished I was, I could never go back to being that person.

Yet I knew no matter how much anger or sadness I could convey to them, it would fall on deaf ears. They didn't understand and would not attempt to simply because they didn't want to. My pain was too uncomfortable for them to acknowledge, and because of that, they wanted me to get over it and pretend that all was well when I was so far away from being fine. I was enraged to be shamed in such a way and was then finally able to pick up Megan's book and find solace in the fact that I wasn't fine. She knew what it was like to feel as if you must continually defend your grief to others who would never understand.

If you look to popular culture to figure out how to tackle grief, you see models that are unrealistic. Devine says, "We believe that grief is a short-term response to a difficult situation, and as such, should be over and done with within a few weeks."[2] Anyone who has experienced grief knows just how bizarre that sounds. When the solid ground under you has shifted in ways that are irreparable, how are we meant to simply pick up the pieces and move along swiftly as if it never happened? Since grief is the reaction to a difficult and often devastating time, we see it as equivalent to being unwell. If we "got over it" and "moved on," we would feel happy and therefore mentally healthy. For me, it was if I was expected to carry on with my life as if nothing had happened. But how could I? Yes, time had passed, but I was still reeling from all my body and mind had gone thorough over the past several months. I had long ago accepted I was sick, but accepting I was no longer ill was much more difficult.

In my battle with cancer and my journey through grief, I remember being told numerous times when I was shown compassion and love that I needed to "soak it all in" and realize that people cared for me, that I was appreciated. I was shocked when those words left someone's lips for my ears to hear. I sat there silently, mumbling that I understood when, really, I was infuriated. Did they really think it took me being diagnosed with cancer to understand that I was loved? Was it being insinuated that, prior to becoming sick, I wasn't appreciative of the people in my life and that somehow I *needed* to become sick to be grateful? How warped is it to think you did something to deserve having cancer?

These statements made me feel as if getting sick was my fault, that somewhere in the universe it was decided I needed to be sick to understand the love and support of my friends and family. If I somehow needed the reminder to appreciate the people in my life, I was sure there were other ways to make it apparent rather than becoming ill to this extent. Devine has said, "You didn't need this thing to happen in order to know what's important, to find your calling, or even to understand that you are, in fact, deeply loved."[3] That hit home for me. I knew I was loved and wasn't in need of the reminder. Rather, I was shown who was going to show up for me in my moments of need, finding those to show up in moments of crisis. My life has taken a sharp detour from my normal life, and I found myself traveling down a new and unfamiliar road to a new destination. It was a road I had to travel alone most of the time, because no matter how much anyone tried to understand my situation, they simply could not.

Devine says telling the truth is essential when discovering a life that feels authentic.[4] This book is my truth. How I managed to survive cancer and the grief that came with it, in all its ugly but real ways.

3

# What about God?

Before I delve into the story of how I found out I had cancer and all that came along with it, it's important to take a minute to talk about religion. During times of crisis, many often turn to religion to find solace. I grew up in a religious household. I was Catholic, so that meant being baptized, receiving the holy communion, and confirmation. It had been years since I had gone to Mass on my own or with my family without it involving a funeral, sad but true. After I received confirmation and was considered an adult in the Catholic community, I went to church less than I had before. I mostly got confirmed because it was what was expected of me to do, and since my older sister hadn't for her own reasons, I felt even more as if I had to, for my family's sake. My relationship with God and church was a complicated one. The idea that God saves people was hard for me to really believe. As a child, I was taught that God took away the pain and the suffering in the world. When it was your time to go, God would appear and take you to the holy land, aka heaven, if you were lucky. This concept sounded nice, but the older I got, the harder it was for me to accept this notion. From 2005 to 2007, I had lost three important people in my life, and based upon what I had been taught to understand, God himself was the reason. He had taken them away from me, which caused my pain and suffering when God was supposed to take away the pain and suffering. At the time, I wasn't thinking about pain and suffering on a global scale, but rather, a personal scale. The world that I lived in every day now hurt in ways it hadn't hurt before.

When the news of my illness spread, one common phrase that was repeated was that I was being prayed for. I wanted to tell them not to waste their breath or thoughts on prayers, primarily because I didn't believe in what has been called the "magic of prayer." Yet I knew if I said my most inner thoughts about prayers to anyone besides my mother, she and my dad would be incredibly embarrassed and hurt because of my religious upbringing, so I faked it. Instead of sharing my true thoughts about their prayers, I would politely thank them, even knowing deep down that prayers weren't going to solve anything or take away the cancer overnight. In my mind, prayer hadn't worked before when people had been taken from my life at an early age, so what was it going to do now?

You can't pray the cancer away or pray people back into existence. Neither prayer nor God were going to take the illness away from me—chemotherapy would. If I believed prayer would solve anything, that meant I was also buying into the idea that the people taken from me in my early life from disease weren't prayed enough for. What did I do that they didn't for the prayers to work for me and not them. I was no one's mother or father. Why did I deserve to get to live? If I wanted to, I could have gone down this rabbit hole looking for justification that there was some earned karma coming back to get me and that's why I got sick. I could have tried to justify why I was getting better and others getting worse as because I had unfinished business to attend to. But doesn't everyone?

There's some force out there, and things happen that we can't fully understand, things that are unexplainable, but I don't believe that there's someone, such as a godly figure, out there deciding our every move and fate for us. I don't believe in a figure that could determine which of us gets to live and which must die. This creates an incorrect dichotomy between those who are blessed and those who aren't. This dichotomy suggests that some are better than others and deserve more of a chance to live, which sounds warped, so naturally, I don't want to buy into it. Logically thinking, was I blessed more than others in my position, or were they damned more than I? There's no way to answer that question, and if it is done, there's no way to justify it. This is a narrative I don't support as I did when I was a child. So, if you prayed for me, I still thank you, just now you know I didn't deserve them more than others, nor do I think it changed anything.

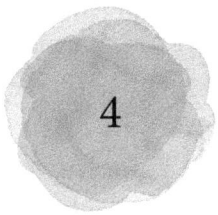

# We All Know Someone

It's a simple fact. In life, we all know someone who has had cancer. It could be anyone from any facet of your life. Long before I was diagnosed with cancer, I'd seen it run through various parts of my own family and beyond. In my own extended family, both of my grandfathers and two of my maternal uncles had cancer. My maternal grandfather died shortly before I was born, and my paternal grandfather died when I was eight years old. On the other hand, both of my uncles are still alive, and throughout their individual battles with the disease, I never would have suspected they were sick because they didn't look or act "sick." Then again, what's a sick person supposed to look like?

This all changed when my mom's best friend and later my best friend's mom were both diagnosed with cancer several years apart. Their cancers were different—they moved quickly. The vibrant, full of life, and colorful women they had been started to disappear quickly. The cancer moved fast, and in only a matter of months, they were gone. Both times, I felt excruciating pain and sadness. This is grief.

In between these two women in my life getting and subsequently dying from cancer, my own mother was diagnosed with cancer in October 2010, my first year of high school. At this time, the only people I was consciously aware of who had cancer had died. And so inside of me, I was afraid my own mom was going to die before my eyes, slowly withering away to nothing. That fear was too strong to ignore. I was in fight-or-flight mode, and I flew, keeping my distance from my mom until she had completed radiation and surgery a few months later. This is grief. Before I knew how to work through it, there was a lot of anger and depression, which is grief. I was angry that people I loved, cornerstones of my life, had gotten sick and died because of it. I was angry that cancer existed. Suddenly, I was meant to continue living when there was a hole in my life that would never be filled the same way ever again. This is grief.

To watch someone, you love wither away to almost nothing is too high a price to pay, yet it is experienced by so many. A cancer diagnosis is the worst news you can get, and then you must take that news and deliver it to others. On June 21, 2022, it became my burden to place onto family and friends. After a long road, I was finally diagnosed with Hodgkin's lymphoma. A week later, after a PET scan, I received the news it was stage 4. I had just turned twenty-six in April, and now I had cancer. In that one moment before my doctor told me the news and the next moment, my life had completely changed, and I'd never be the same person I was before. What a hard pill to swallow.

This pill was made harder to swallow when the news was broken to family and friends, and they brought what was thought to be helpful and inspiring information but which was quite irritating. Suddenly, everyone I knew had met someone who had Hodgkin's lymphoma, or a family member had it, and they'd lived. It suddenly seemed as if I were receiving texts or calls from people either telling me how sorry they were or how they'd met and got to talking about me, at which point I was desperate to end the phone call or ignore the text. I, for one, didn't like being talked about. I didn't think everyone, and anyone needed to know my personal business of having been diagnosed with cancer. I also didn't want to hear stories about those who had previously been in my shoes, and all was well.

I had just been hit with the worst news imaginable and hearing how it would turn out all right. Everyone has a different response to cancer and the treatment he or she receives, and I didn't want to be placed in the category of *all right*, because in my mind nothing about this was all right. On one occasion, I was given the name and phone number to someone a friend had met who'd survived the disease in, case I had any questions or wanted to talk to someone. I knew everyone meant well, but the last thing I wanted to hear was that I wasn't alone and that there were others out there that understood. The truth was, I was alone, and no one, even if he or she had been through it and survived, could understand me and what I was feeling.

Even those who had been through the same type of cancer I had would never fully understand what I was going through, physically, mentally, and emotionally. I was in early grief at the rawest and most vulnerable point, and the last thing I wanted was to be comforted. There was no comfort to be found—no words could "fix" what was broken. I didn't need to be fixed. I desperately needed to come up for air but was suffocated by the words of others. These words of comfort felt bad because knowing someone else had suffered in this way wasn't a comfort. Rather, it was a nightmare knowing another woman's life that been drastically shattered and altered—it didn't bring any relief.

Devine describes how "help" from others can feel like an intrusion. Many attempts at making connections don't come across the way they intend to, but rather as clueless.[4] This is exactly what I felt. I knew they wanted me to find hope in knowing others who had this disease and beat it, but there was no hope for me at this point. I didn't want to feel connected to those who had cancer. It wasn't a group I ever wanted to be a part of, and I didn't need any more reminders that I was. I had cancer and wanted to shut myself away from the outside world and any words of comfort. I was deeply angry, and no matter how well intentioned their thoughts and actions were, I was feeling robbed of what Devine calls the "central importance of our individual reality." The reality of who I was and the life I was living vanished into thin air.

# Meeting My Grief

5

# Diagnosed

It had been a full year since the first lockdown from COVID-19, and around me, different people in my life had fallen ill with COVID, coworkers, children in my care, family members, but I had been lucky to not catch it myself. This was until Martin Luther King Jr. Day. I was getting ready to go to lunch with friends and was suffering from a sore throat and slight cough. If it hadn't been for my sister telling me I should test before I went, I never would have and could have passed it onto others without ever knowing it. Until I tested positive, I thought I was coming down with either strep throat or a sinus infection. I was lucky to not have lost my sense of smell or taste. I quarantined and continued to wear a mask in public afterward.

As the months went on following this run-in, my cough persisted, and my primary care physician, Dr. Mikloucich, told me that certain symptoms, including cough, could be expected to stay for at least twelve weeks if not longer after testing positive. There was just so much unknown about the long-term effects of the disease; so I was just going along with what my doctor had to say. That isn't to say I didn't keep an eye on it to see if it ever got worse. Eventually, the cough went away with time, but other changes in my body were occurring that I attributed to having had COVID, that it took months for me to bring it up to a doctor.

Throughout the years I have struggled to sleep, I was able to fall asleep, but staying asleep was the issue. The struggle I was now facing wasn't that of being able to fall asleep, but rather, I couldn't stay asleep because I was being woken up completely drenched in sweat. I would either simply change from one pair of shorts and T-shirt and go back to sleep or shower in the middle of the night—it was that bad. Sometimes I could still feel my wet sheets beneath me as I would go back to bed. Thinking about that now grosses me out. It was late winter in upstate New York, so I assumed I was in too many layers of clothing with too many blankets on top, causing my body to overheat. I thought I was a deep enough sleep that my body couldn't warn me I was too warm until enough sweat had left my body to begin to cool itself down.

Months later, I would discover that in fact I wasn't overheating, but rather, I was feverish and sweating because my fever had broken. When I woke up, the thought of being in layers of clothing or blankets was no longer an option. I was much too warm. In the moment, it never occurred to me to take my temperature. I was mostly concerned with getting in dry clothes and going back to sleep. Throughout the day, I didn't feel sick or cold to the point where I thought I had a fever. Everything that was happening was happening during the night, so no one else knew, and I'd wake up in the morning, feel fine, and go to work without any problems.

Right after having COVID, I was becoming a long-term substitute for a teacher on family leave in the classroom that would inevitably become mine. I was working full-time and making it through the days without struggling health-wise. It was only on the weekends that my exhaustion became apparent. I would go to sleep by nine o'clock at night and sleep soundlessly through the night, minus the occasional intermission from night sweats, to wake up the next morning late into the morning or early afternoon. I've never been one to sleep in, but now, I'd sleep till eleven o'clock or later. My parents would come check on me to make sure I was okay because I was sound asleep. After I awoke, I would make something for breakfast, and that wiped me out again, so I would go back to sleep until the evening. Sure enough, I'd manage to eat dinner, shower, and go back to sleep for the night. For weeks and weeks, I never brought up my exhaustion to a doctor because I thought it was a long-term effect of COVID, or I thought maybe I had mono as well, and doctors couldn't do anything about. If I had mono or was experiencing lasting effects of COVID, I assumed that my fatigue would go away on its own, as my cough had, so I thought I'd just wait it out.

Despite wanting to wait it out, different people noticed my extreme exhaustion and began to question it. If I managed to go anywhere after work, I always rested my head on my arms, ready to drift off. At this point, my dad encouraged me to go to my doctor to see if there was a way to find out what was really going on and see if there was a way to make the situation better. Before I could get an appointment to see Dr. Mikloucich, I saw my dermatologist for a regular check-in with my acne-prone sensitive skin and the routine I was following via her directions and prescriptions. She would become the catalyst to discovering the underlying cause of all that was occurring to me.

I, like many others, have experienced bad acne for years. I first started to see a dermatologist when I was fourteen years old. My acne was on my face and my back, which made me very self-conscious, especially in the beginning of my high school years. This dermatologist was a man, and I always felt as if he never understood my struggle with acne and what it caused me mentally. I was very self-conscious about the acne and felt that if I could see it, so could others, despite my attempts to cover it up. I was prescribed a topical ointment to use in combination with a medicated pad and benzol peroxide wash in the shower. Over many years, I received various topical treatments, some prescriptions and other over-the-counter medications. I went through at least three dermatologists over twelve years until I saw on Facebook a friend looking for dermatology recommendations and someone had commented about Anew Dermatology in Johnson City, New York.

I was extremely discouraged with the results I had previously gotten. It always seemed as if the dermatologists I had gone to were overbooked and didn't really have the time to sit down with me to understand my skin concerns and take more than a thirty-second passing look at my skin. Not this time, though. I was immediately sold on Julie Luckman. She took the time to sit and listen to the struggles I had faced with previous dermatologists and treatment plans. Within this first appointment I was told I had sensitive skin, which I had never previously known. Over the past dozen years, I had been doing more damage to my skin than good because I had never known my accurate skin type. Right away, I began a treatment that seemed to work, using a combination of low-dose prescription topical medications and over-the-counter sensitive-skin face wash and lotion.

Just as the acne of my body cleared up and the small red pimples on my face got better, the large, painful, stubborn, hormonal acne didn't seem to budge. At least, it ebbed and flowed along my menstrual cycle, which other women can relate to. It got to the point where my dermatologist wanted to prescribe the medication Accutane but couldn't because I was anemic. Accutane has been known to cause anemia, and Julie wanted the approval of Dr. Mikloucich before starting me on the medication. This was no surprise to me. I've always been anemic. Even Dr. Mikloucich was aware of it, so I figured I would see her and get the approval without an issue. Then I could start Accutane.

But in life, we're thrown curveballs, and getting my iron in check would be no simple feat.

Dr. Mikloucich didn't give me the approval I needed to start Accutane. Turns out I was severely anemic, and she wanted to see my iron levels increase before starting Julie's plan for my skin. I tried taking various oral iron supplements and had my blood drawn weekly for about a month, but nothing worked. I was still anemic; my body wasn't absorbing the iron, whether it was over the counter or prescription strength. The lack of iron and inability to absorb it with a pill meant I was referred to hematology for iron infusions. Dr. Mikloucich seemed confident this was the cause of the exhaustion I was having since iron levels are intrinsically linked to our energy levels.

At the beginning of May, reversing my anemia with hematology should have been an easy fix, which normally means it was not. I met the wonderful Dr. Jessica Hals, who also thought this was going to be an easy fix. We met and went forward with doing two iron infusions. I went to the hospital, in the back room of the hematology/oncology department, where cancer patients were receiving chemotherapy. The iron was infused through an IV. It was easy and painless.

About a week after my second infusion, I went to the emergency room because I couldn't poop. Years prior, I had been taking iron supplements and was told to stop because I was also having gastrointestinal problems at the time, suffering from either constipation or diarrhea. This doctor suggesting the oral iron supplements as the root cause. Here I was, about two if not three years later, and once again, I was experiencing constipation because of iron. However, this kind of iron was the highly concentrated kind, which was directly pumped into my veins to be absorbed. I was experiencing extreme pain in my stomach, doubled over from the inability to make a bowel movement, and I was trying everything I could think of to help me go to the bathroom. I took a fiber supplement daily, drank water mixed with MiraLAX, drank kombucha, and so on, and nothing seemed to work. I would go a little, but never enough for a fraction of the pain to go away.

At this point, the fluctuating fevers that only occurred in the middle of the night while I was sleeping slowly began recurring in the evening while I was awake. They started as low grade around 99.5 degrees. I knew something was wrong, so at first, I went to the walk-in. While there, an X-ray was taken showed a bowel blockage. I was given two options: wait and see if it passed or go to the emergency room. Hours passed, and my pain only seemed to increase, so off to the emergency room I went. It was late, and it would be hours until I was spoken to and eventually sent home.

On this night, June 1, I was never looked at by a doctor, but my information, vitals, blood, and a urine sample were taken. After waiting for hours in the waiting room, it was closing in on midnight, and a doctor still hadn't come to see me. Eventually, one came out to the waiting room to speak to me, and I was given a dose of Senokot in the triage room that night, and two prescriptions were sent to my pharmacy for me. I was told these laxatives should work in twenty-four to forty-eight hours. My fever was never addressed that night, and I felt brushed off. My body was telling me something was wrong, and I wasn't being taken seriously. I felt as if it was simply stemming from the fact that I was constipated.

Forty-eight hours passed, and, lo and behold, the different laxatives I had been prescribed had done nothing. I still hadn't gone to the bathroom. Back to the emergency room I went, and this time, it was a different story. I had taken my temperature at home, and it turned out to be a whopping 100.5 degrees. They could no longer ignore it. Now I had proper imaging done to supplement the one X-ray that had been taken days prior. The results weren't great. I had an infection in my bowel from a blockage of stool. Gross, I know. On top of that, there was fluid in my right lung and around my heart. Two areas of the body where fluid should not be.

That night—or should I say, early morning—I was admitted to a four-day stay at Lourdes Hospital. In those four days, I had more blood drawn from my body than I thought would have been possible, plus some wonderful antibiotics that caused my veins to burn because they were so strong. During this time, I had other imaging tests done as various doctors attempted to make sense of what was going on inside my body. At one point, an infectious disease doctor thought I had an autoimmune disease, such as Lyme disease or lupus. That didn't scare me. They were survivable, and I could live with them if that were the case. If you haven't figured it out yet, Lyme disease and lupus weren't the cases. The antibiotics began to tackle the infection, and when I could finally go to the bathroom again, I was ready to leave. One slight problem arose, though. They didn't have an answer to what exactly was wrong. You don't get a fluid buildup in and around your heart and lungs like that because you're constipated.

During my four-day stay at the hospital, an ultrasound was performed to get a clearer image for a better understanding of the fluid around my heart. They couldn't figure what was causing it. At the same time, I had a full liter of cloudy yellow liquid removed from my right lung. The fluid was tested, and the initial results came back negative for an autoimmune disease, no Lyme disease or lupus detected. I was happy with the outcome, but I could tell my parents weren't exactly thrilled. Still, I suspected that I could leave the hospital without having any serious issues. I would continue to take the antibiotics, and the fluid that remained around my heart would sort itself out. Again, not the best decision, but the doctors did say more test results would come in from the fluid that had been removed from my lung in three to five days. If anything had come back positive, they would let me know. I never received word about a positive test result.

I went back to my everyday life, living as if nothing had happened or changed because no one had an answer, and I wasn't necessarily looking for one at the time. Naturally, that changed once I got a massage after spending four restless days and nights in an uncomfortable hospital bed. My wonderful massage therapist, Karen, whom I have known for years, asked me if I knew that the lymph nodes on my neck were swollen. I had no idea. Even the doctors at the hospital hadn't noticed. I knew there was a lump in my left armpit, but I had just started using a new deodorant because the one I usually use had run out and it was all I had at the time, so I figured I was just having an allergic reaction. It hadn't been looked at much at the hospital, and no tests had been done on it. Again, I thought it was something that would resolve itself with time. Moral of this story, when it comes to your health and well-being, never trust something to simply sort itself out unless you're a doctor or know what you're doing, because I'm not a doctor, I didn't know what I was doing, and in my case, it didn't sort itself out.

Luckily for me, the day after I received this massage, I was going to see Dr. Mikloucich, as it's customary to see your doctor after a multiple day stay in the hospital. I went in with confidence, still believing nothing was severely wrong, a bit optimistic for myself if I'm being honest. I was glad to know she wasn't convinced that I had an autoimmune disease because of the lack of support for this diagnosis from any test results she'd received from the fluid that had been drained. Still, she did her due diligence and sent me that same afternoon back to the hospital to get ultrasounds of the swollen lymph nodes on both sides of my neck and armpit.

This is when things began to move quickly. It was a Friday afternoon when the ultrasounds were done, and before I left the hospital after the imaging had been completed, Dr. Mikloucich had set an appointment up for that Monday. I was going to see surgeon about a biopsy. We're nearing the middle of June, which means it is getting quite warm. The most logical way to prevent an infection at the biopsy sight and get the best possible sample was to biopsy the largest lymph node that was located on the right side of my neck. This was done the very next day. Again, I went back to life as normal at work, getting ready for the end of the school year and the beginning of summer camp. I was getting slightly more conscious that something could be wrong, but not to the point where I was worried. I was mostly focused on how to remove the purple marker used to indicate the precise location of where the biopsy would be done.

Exactly one week after the biopsy was completed, I was at work when I got the phone call from Dr. Mikloucich. It was a Tuesday, midmorning or just after noon, and I had already missed the call from the surgeon with my biopsy results. I bet you're wondering how I could have missed that call. It was the preschool graduation, and I oversaw announcing the students' names as they graduated. I immediately went outside once I had completed my duties and saw that I had a missed call from the surgeon. I returned the call but unfortunately just missed the doctor, who had gone back into surgery It would be at least another hour if not more until he was free to now return my call. So, when I saw Dr. Mikloucich come up on my caller ID, I would not risk missing receiving my test results for a second time.

I got up from where I was sitting and went into our maintenance man's office. I could tell by her voice something was wrong. She wasn't cheerful but sounded somber. The diagnosis came. I was told I had Hodgkin's lymphoma. I went numb. I heard her, but at the same time, I kept thinking it couldn't be true, even though I knew there was no mistake made, and in my head, I had come to some sort of peace knowing I could have cancer. But I still didn't want it to be a reality I had to face.

After I got off the phone, the hard part came. I would take being told I had cancer any day over now having to share the news with my loved ones, now placing a burden on their shoulders because I was sick. First, I made a three-way phone call with my mom and sister. I left it up to my mom to tell my dad, he had been driving and was more than halfway to Florida at this point. He'd just bought a home-inspection business down there, and I couldn't be the bearer of sad news. In that tiny office, time had frozen. It was quiet, and I was still in a state of shock that hit full force when I went back into the hallway where life was moving on around me as if nothing had changed. And nothing had for anyone else. Only my world had just blown apart, and I, for the most part, had to carry on with my day as if it hadn't.

I went back into the office of my boss, Karen, shut the door and the sliding glass piece that covered the window to tell her the news. She hugged me, and we both cried. Next, I told Victoria and Robin, both of whom I work with and who had followed along with every step of this process, continually asking how I was doing and if I had any news. I was in a bubble within a bubble. First was a work bubble, separate from my family and other close friends, and then a second was a small bubble of people who knew there, and I needed to expand that to two of my best friends. We're long-distance friends, and this wasn't the news I could tell them over text. Slowly, I worked through telling those in my innermost circle between phone calls, FaceTimes, and one in person until I could no longer bear to see people's faces or hear their voices when I told them. So, I ended up texting my best friends from high school, and that was that for now. Shortly after, I told others at work, and my mom told my family on my behalf.

I was now entering a period where I would have to tell my story over and over. I was not only having to tell my diagnosis but also what led up to it to anyone who had known about my sweating and exhaustion or those who were stunned that someone like me could have cancer "out of the blue." Nothing really happens out of the blue. There were warning signs, and I ignored mine. I was now living with the consequences of this decision and retelling the story not only to others but also to myself as well, over, and over in my mind. Devine calls this "telling the story." We are trained as humans to be storytellers, and the compulsion not only to tell the story but also to relive it is a coping mechanism. It's one which we use to hope that the ending of the story will change over time, even though it never does change the outcome.

Now that I had answers the real work began. I was unaware at the time, but this was the beginning of my journey through grief and all the discomfort it would cause.

6

# Five Letters

G-R-I-E-F, grief, a five-letter word with its five distinct stages, denial, anger, bargaining, depression, and acceptance. Everyone has had a run-in with grief at one point or another in his or her life. The movement in and out of these stages occurs when something traumatic has happened in our lives resulting in the loss of someone. Grief is an individual experience. No one's is the same. Yet it can happen to people simultaneously. Traumatic events have happened in my life repeatedly, but this time, it was different. All the other times it had occurred because something had happened in my life, but not directly to me or my body. My previous experience with grief was because of a death in my family and my trauma response to it. Not now. No one had physically died, but there was a death within, and I had to live with it.

In one instant, one breath, everything was different. Everything had changed. A coldness set in, and an intense numbness spread over my whole body. I was now tasked with facing a battle that I wasn't sure I was going to win. I went into survival mode. I had become more important to myself than ever before, and I placed myself, my thoughts, and feelings at the top of my priority list. I knew others would have their own opinions and emotions about my diagnosis, their own grief. As selfish as it might seem, I didn't care. I couldn't care. It didn't matter what anyone had to say. I was the one who was sick, the one whose entire life had been thrown off its tracks. A commitment to myself was made the day I was diagnosed. I had to continuously put myself above others to get through this. I thought I needed to be a lone wolf to be able to fully process and understand how my body was attacking itself and how I had been ignoring it for months.

I've always been someone who liked to work alone and get things done my way, which isn't to say I can't work with others but that I'm more of a leader than a follower. Therefore, I was fully prepared to face portions of this battle alone, I almost preferred it to be that way at times. Yet I knew I wasn't going to have to do it alone. I had family, friends, and coworkers to lean on, but there was just part of what I was going to go through that I needed to do for myself by myself. Surrounded by my own feelings and emotions, I didn't want to show people how I was feeling. I wanted to keep it to myself and show those around me that I could handle all that was happening.

When grief begins, there's no magic signal or notification that you've entered it. Often, we deny that we're in denial because the pain is too intense and we can't imagine giving into it. I had no idea I was grieving until I was nearing the end of my battle with cancer. In the middle of trying to survive, I had lost myself.

The representation I saw throughout popular media of a cancer-stricken patient was someone in the hospital throughout the duration of their treatment, pale and bald, or going to group meetings to bond with those in comparable situations. I knew right off the bat that I wasn't interested in any type of support group with strangers. As a child, no one in my family that I knew to have had cancer appeared that sick to me or went to support groups, but everyone had his or her own secrets. That all changed when my mom's best friend, who I called ZeeZeeZella, and later my best friend's mom, Mama Sullivan, as I called her, appeared to me in that sickly way. The types of cancer they had were different, and they were diagnosed while I was in two completely distinct stages in my life—ZeeZeeZella when I was in adolescence and Mama Sullivan when I was a teenager. The one thing their cancers had in common was that they moved quickly. These two women who had been so full of light and love had begun to fade in front of my eyes, and as much as I knew why, I still couldn't understand why it was happening to them. In only a matter of months, they were gone. The excruciating pain and sadness I felt during those times is something I will never forget. This is grief.

In between those instances, my own mother was diagnosed with cancer. She was lucky; she survived. When she told me she was sick, I ran out of my house barefoot to a friend who lived a block away. I couldn't face the truth. I couldn't see my own mother fade away as I had with both ZeeZeeZella and Mama Sullivan, the two other motherly figures I had in my life. My trauma response was flight. This is grief.

The grief I felt through those situations was nothing compared to the grief I found myself facing after my diagnosis. It wasn't an automatic overnight discovery that I was grieving, because so much is going on at once. The reality was that I wasn't just dealing with my own emotions but with those of family and friends as well. The constant flow of messages delivered to me via different modes of communication was a lot to take in all at once. I hardly had a moment to think for myself and truly begin to process the steps I had to take to get diagnosed, including going back to the emergency room several times when I knew something wasn't right, but different doctors had no answer. I was also grappling with the thoughts of what I would inevitably have to go through over the course of my treatment over the next few months. Before I knew it, grief had started to settle itself in, and it began with anger, lots of anger.

# 7

# Red

Everyone has walked into a room, and suddenly, the room goes silent. You know they were just discussing you, but no one will admit it, and you don't know what was said. That's how I felt. I knew that everyone in my day-to-day life and beyond was talking about me and my situation. I felt like I was in a fishbowl, just trying to go about my life in a way that was as normal as possible when others were gawking at me. I wanted to hide away from the world because I didn't want to talk to anyone.

Everyone wanted to know how I was. The answer was, "Not great," but I wasn't going to admit it and go into a sob story about the unfortunate circumstance that suddenly surrounded my life, because nothing they said or did would change the situation. The sentiment that I got the most, which simultaneously unnerved me the most, was that people were praying for me. I quickly could no longer stand to hear those words. That is all well and good, and some might believe in the power of prayer, I wasn't one of those people. I kept thinking how prayers could help me, especially when I wasn't one to turn to religion when things got tough.

The feeling of being watched was also mixed with anger, disappointment, frustration, and impatience. All became standard after my initial diagnosis and over the next several months. I desperately wanted answers, and I wanted to do it alone. I was so overwhelmed with emotions, information, and what seemed to be life-or-death decisions that I let this irritability I was feeling grow until I would inevitably explode. More than anything, I felt defeated. An emotion that I had previous experience with, but now it would become synonymous with my cancer battle. I had to continuously try to grasp what was happening in an ever-changing war within my own body, which always felt abstract and distant. I felt it throughout every fiber in my body, and it would ebb and flow throughout the days as they rolled by. Just as the defeat would come and go, pure anger would too. It came quickly and would linger before inevitably going. Each time it did, I knew it had to be taken for what it was without dwelling on the day prior and worrying about what was yet to come, but that was just as demanding on my mind as the anger was.

When I think about colors associated with feelings, red automatically appears when I think about anger. In my life, I've had flashes of anger in various aspects of life, but now it was always lurking around every corner waiting for the right moment to strike. When I couldn't let it slip, it sank lower and lower into my own feelings about myself. The anger lurked everywhere, at home with my family, at work, and at the doctors. I was absolutely dumbfounded that I wasn't diagnosed earlier. I kept replaying the previous six months in my head all the way back to January, trying to make it make sense in my mind, but I couldn't.

My mind raced nonstop as I thought of all the symptoms I had been showing, various doctors I had seen, tests that had been done, and I couldn't stop. Not one of the doctors or nurses or any medical professional I had gone to for months realized that I was this ill. I was getting bloodwork done every single week for months, and nothing looked off to them. That boggled my mind and, to this day, almost seems unfathomable. I had been to the walk-in and seen my primary care doctor, a physical therapist, and lastly, my oncologist, who at the time was only treating me for anemia. The fact of the matter was that not a single person had recognized something was wrong when the signs were there. I knew I couldn't blame anyone for not finding the cancer sooner, but the anger I felt told me that someone needed to be blamed, and it was them. At age twenty-six, stage 4 cancer was in every part of my lymphatic system, and I was not only enraged but also numb.

It was as if there were too many emotions going on at once to really feel or differentiate one from the other. I was aware of the emotions of others around me, but those weren't my responsibility to deal with. I didn't want to see anyone, didn't want to look in the mirror, and didn't want to talk about it. There was no need. I had cancer, end of story, what more was there to say. Still, I desperately needed to talk about it and cry, just let the tears fall until they stopped, but I wouldn't let myself feel. Allowing myself to feel it and talk about it made it real, and I didn't want to believe it was happening, not to me, not so young, not at all. This is avoidance, and I had become good at it.

The only way I could make any of what was going on inside of me make sense was to take the anger I was really feeling toward myself and place it elsewhere while projecting it onto those closest to me. I could barely manage what I was feeling, let alone the people around me. As soon as I was diagnosed, I was ready to enter the arena, so to speak, and get it over with. I thought it would give me something to grasp onto and give pause to my racing thoughts. I didn't have any questions. I was ready, no second opinion necessary.

The same couldn't be said for my family. The numbness left my body as soon as they started asking the doctor about going to get a second opinion and about different clinical trials. I had never been so angry in my life. Here we were at *my* appointment because I was the one who had cancer, and there they were, asking questions about things they wanted. Not once had anyone looked to me and asked if I wanted to go to another facility and get a second opinion or if I had even thought about participating in a clinical trial. In fact, if they had asked, they would have known that I wanted neither of those things. I barely wanted to schlep to the doctors here, let alone hours away, more outside of my comfort zone, for them to run the exact same tests and come to the same result but at the expense of my already-deteriorating health.

Of course, I couldn't say anything to them in the room, so I politely bit my tongue, looked at my oncologist, and said, "We won't be doing any of that." Now once we had left the office, which was a different story, I let my family have it. Sure, they were going through their own emotions and feelings about me being sick, which I understood, I know they only wanted what was best for me. I should have assumed they would have their own questions, but in my stubborn mind, it wasn't about them and what they wanted. We made a deal. If they were to come to appointments in the future, they had to run all questions past me first, and if I didn't want to bring it up, it wouldn't be brought up. This might sound a bit harsh, but it was the way I needed to deal with it. If there's ever a time to be selfish in life, it is when you've been diagnosed with cancer.

Once chemotherapy had started, my body just wasn't the same anymore. I felt different. It's hard to describe exactly what it felt like, but I knew something was off. It wasn't nausea. I wasn't dizzy/ I felt the opposite, like I was glowing. A buzzing feeling ran through my veins as the medicine worked its magic. Just as objects lost their shine, the buzzing feeling left, along with the glow by nightfall and there I was again, back to being myself while not being myself at all. The feeling of being a superhero defeating the bad within left, and I transformed back into myself and would crumble.

In my prior life, I had been able to work a full eight-hour day and power through like it was nothing, not anymore. Now I could barely handle going up and down the stairs multiple times a day. Suddenly, I had to rely on others more often for things I could have previously done, which seemed almost foreign to me. I'm lucky I had such understanding coworkers that were all willing to pitch in and help whenever needed, but I still didn't always like it because it made me feel insufficient, as if I wasn't doing enough. Naturally, this frustrated me, and I went home bone tired from the frustration that was low in my belly to cry in the few moments where I found myself alone and could let it all go.

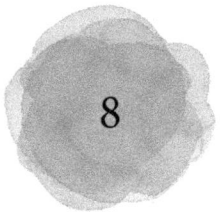

8

# Hair Wars

Hair is one of the most important accessories someone can have or own. Whether it is short, long, wavy, straight, curly, thick, or thin, it's intrinsically part of what makes us us. To some, hair might seem superficial, but when you have none, it turns into something that seems all too significant. I remember looking in the mirror and feeling as if the hair I had was just hanging from my head like a dead thing. I've always had straight hair, and I had worked tremendously hard at getting it to a healthy length after years of bathroom dye jobs in high school. Since I was young, my dad had always said that girls with curly hair straighten it and those with straight hair curl it. This was true. My hair was straight, and for just about every formal occasion I would attempt to curl it, even though it had never exactly turned out as I had wished it had; the curl wouldn't last no matter what I tried. It's as if we can't be happy with what we are given.

As soon as I found out I was going to lose my hair, I made the decision to have it shaved before chemotherapy had even begun. In my initial appointment right after diagnosis, my oncologist explained that, about two to three weeks after my second treatment, the hair would start to fall out. Realistically, I knew this was a strong possibility, but it hits differently when you're told it's a reality you will soon have to face. Hearing it aloud and not just some abstract thought in my own head was a low blow. I wasn't afraid of losing my hair per se, because I knew it would grow back. What scared me was how it would come out.

Clumps. My long, beautiful hair was going to fall out in clumps. Not smoothly or evenly, but in patchy clumps leaving scattered chunks missing from my scalp. I could just touch my hair and have it fall out in my hands. Instead of a few strands, large chunks would come out in the shower. I would wake up with it scattered across my pillows and sheets. This petrified me to my core. I couldn't shake the thought of being out in public somewhere and end up having a clump of hair in my hands and a random bald spot on my scalp with no way to hide it. Picturing a day where I woke up surrounded by hair that had fallen out overnight wasn't something I thought I could bear. I didn't want to wake up to the horror of it. Any hair-related nightmares that I had never crossed my mind until now were suddenly at the forefront of my thoughts, and the only way to shake them was to do away with the root cause, my hair.

Keeping my hair and watching it disappear or getting rid of it on my terms were my only two options, and neither was exactly what I wanted. Yet I opted for the second option, and this wasn't as easy a decision as it may seem. The sheer thought of slowly watching my hair disappear day after day not only saddened but also angered me enough to shave my head before I even started treatment. I loved my hair; it was part of who I was. Sometimes, even now, I wish I hadn't done it. Hell, I still wish I never had been able to lose any hair at all, but that wasn't the reality I was facing. In that moment, I had a decision to make: let the chemo take it or me. I was in a whirlwind of information, thoughts, and feelings, and my hair seemed to be the one and only thing I had any kind of tangible control over.

My wonderful friend Sara and her sister Chrissy, who is my hairdresser, shaved my head for me. They were the only people I trusted to make what was a bitter and heartbreaking situation easier. Instead of being dismal, it was as pleasurable as it could be. They gave me a bob, bangs, and many different hairstyles in between so I could try out other styles I may not have thought of prior. Sara made the first cut. She couldn't mess it up—no one was going to see it. Despite this life-changing somber event, there wasn't a tear in sight. I felt empowered. I was able to take control of this one part of the journey I was on. It was the only thing I could say cancer didn't take from me, because I'd made the decision myself. It was the best feeling, and I used that feeling to share with the world, my world, that I was sick. The outpouring of love and messages I received was incredibly heartwarming. That made me cry, and so did my own reflection in the mirror when I got home that night and had no hair.

After my first head shaving, I was enthralled by the feeling of my buzzed head. It was a sensation I had never experienced with my own hair before. I couldn't stop rubbing my head. Despite the satisfaction I had, every time I rubbed my head, I was reminded that I had no hair. I became hyperfocused on the image in my head of what I thought I looked like and, thus, what I must have looked like to others. The image in my head wasn't pretty—she wasn't me.

Regardless of this, there was still a small bright side to having no hair in June. It was a scorching summer, so not having long hair that would hang down my back was a relief. Taking control of my life in that way felt very freeing. In one instance, I had lost control of everything in my life except my own reaction. I chose to take a stand and say I was ready to go head-to-head with this disease and come out on the other side victorious. Shaving my head early was my way to signify that not only to myself but also to anyone who saw me.

That still didn't make it easy. Immediately, I felt powerful, with adrenaline coursing through my veins, but that effect wore off quickly. There are only so many times you can be told you have the right kind of head to have no hair. Not too big or too round. At first, it was nice to hear the support and compliments; it reaffirmed that I had made the right decision. I went back and reread the supportive comments on the original Facebook post I'd made about my diagnosis, and the initial feeling of empowerment came back. Despite this, the feeling wouldn't last. Every time I saw my true reflection in a mirror, I was reminded of the life I was now living and the sadness I felt.

I was hearing how good I looked, how brave I was, and how amazing it was that I was doing this all while working, but in my own head, there was a lot of negativity and second-guessing. I went from being diagnosed to shaving my head all within a week, not allowing myself a lot of time to process what was happening. I couldn't help but wonder if I had made the right decision and not just about my hair. I had a million different thoughts bouncing around in my head, giving me mental whiplash. Should I have been working through this? Should I have taken time off? If I took time off, what would I have done, where would I have gone? Nowhere was the answer, because I was sick and couldn't travel without the risk of catching something with my weakened immune system. I needed the money, and it provided a distraction from my newfound reality, so I went when I could push through the pain. I still question if that was the right thing to do.

The questioning continued day after day in my own head, never spoken aloud because I didn't want anyone to know I was struggling like this. There was a lot of distaste when I saw my own reflection. I didn't feel like myself, I didn't look like myself, and I wasn't me anymore. Suddenly, clothes didn't look right on my body, and it wasn't just because I had lost some weight. The dresses felt abnormal; makeup no longer sat right on my face. It was as if all the femininity I had just vanished. How could I feel like a woman with no hair when it has been drilled into my brain the way to be feminine and a woman was to have long, flowing, luscious hair and the little I had left was the complete opposite?

As much as I wanted my doctor to be wrong, she was not. A few weeks after my second treatment, I was driving from one appointment to another, and while I absentmindedly rubbed my shaven head, the little bit of hair I had left fell out in my hands. I began to cry; slowly, hot burning tears ran down my face while I sat at the red light, mourning the last bits of my former self that were leaving my body.

The struggles I found within this new body of mine were ones that I had never dealt with so intensely before. I had no hair to hide a scar on my neck from the biopsy and a scar right above my port that stuck out on the right side of my chest, which I so badly tried to hide beneath clothes. So much was new and different to me all at once, and it was hard to keep up. One day, clothes fit me, and I felt great, and the next day, things didn't sit quite right, and I could do nothing about it but put them away and hope the next items of clothing I put on not only fit but also looked better too. I couldn't wear clothes that I wanted because I didn't look like me anymore. It was like I was looking at my reflection in a warped fun house mirror. I wasn't and what I saw was an awkward uncomfortable person staring back at me.

The joy I had when I'd first made the decision to shave my head wore off, and I was desperate and willing enough to do about anything to get some kind of hair back on my head, including getting a wig. Even though the desperation was there, finding a wig was impossible, especially a high quality one that wasn't extremely expensive. The moment I first felt the little bit of hair I had falling out was when I went into a now-or-never scenario. I needed to find a wig in that moment, or it would be over for me. I had never felt panic like that before. So, what did I do? I made an appointment at one of the only wig stores in my area that I had heard of and spent over four hundred dollars out of pocket on a blond shoulder-length wig with a lot more volume than I had ever experienced with my natural hair. To make it worse, I didn't like the wig. It was simply the best option out of the ones I had tried on, and I was so petrified of not having one I went with it. To make matters worse, I wouldn't get reimbursed from my insurance for the wig. Why? Because this salon and wig shop wasn't approved by my insurance. Okay, so what places were? Few. To top it off, the list I got from my insurance company produced a whopping zero that were still in business or sold wigs in my area. I was in utter shock. Again came anger.

I know where I live isn't necessarily a huge city, but I still expected to find at least a few places to at least consider finding a good wig at an affordable price. I had heard I could get a wig for free from the American Cancer Society. I investigated and couldn't find that as an option. I was back to square one, still without hair, and an expensive wig I learned to tolerate for a time. Summer was now winding down, and a new school year was just around the corner. I had my wig cut and learned how to style it to highlight my face.

Just as I was getting used to wearing it, I showed someone who I considered to be important in my life a picture of myself in the wig, expecting them to lift me up; instead, they brought me down. This wig was blond and while I'm a natural blonde, my hair hadn't been that color in a long time. It was also shorter than my natural hair had been in years. More than anything, I wanted an affirmation from that person that I looked as good as I'd grown to think. The opposite happened. They told me they didn't like the wig; therefore, they didn't like me and what I looked like in it. That was all it took for me to look at myself differently once again. It might be easy to think I should not have placed so much on one opinion, but it was one I cared about the most, and I was crushed when I didn't get the result I wanted. The truth hurts. Part of me wished that person had lied and said they liked it. I have not worn that wig since.

In between that and eventually finding a wig I liked, I had a failed attempt at ordering one online from the American Cancer Society. Turns out I didn't like it as much as I thought I did—everything looks better online. Months later, after so much disappointment and anxiety over the way I looked, I made a final effort to find a wig that I liked, to enjoy what I saw in the mirror looking back at me. This is when I went to Paradise Hair World in Binghamton, New York, and was able to find a more affordable wig that I liked.

I went in with less than high hopes about finding something and was riddled with anxiety. One of the women working came and helped me. She explained everything I needed to know about the several types of wigs and made me feel confident in my decision, making my experience a relief. It was vital to have someone as kind and caring as her helping me during one of the lowest points in this journey. The wig was long and brown, more like my own hair than the previous one. The only difference was that the wig was thick and curly, two things I had never experienced with my own natural hair. It was a whole new learning curve I got to experience, which came with its own set of frustrations. When I wanted hair but wanted it up, it seemed impossible. The only way the wig seemed to look right was when some but not all from the front was pulled back away from my face. Wasn't always what I wanted, but it was the best I could get and despite the desire to have a high ponytail or bun, I could make do with what I had. After months of struggle and dissatisfaction, I had what I wanted in a way that made things a little bit better for the time being.

PART THREE

# Mixed Emotions

9

# This Is Not My Body

After I was first diagnosed, I realized I had lost a lot of weight unintentionally. Clothes no longer fit, and things about my body just seemed off. This change became more prominent throughout the summer when I shaved my head and lost the hair I had. Who I was had changed. Without realizing it, I had built a lot of who I was around what I looked like. I'd thought I was pretty, not anymore. I lost my femininity. It hurt. I hated who I saw in the mirror, and no matter how much I tried to avoid them, I still saw my reflection and was angry. I was angry that I had turned into who I became. I was angry that, no matter what I tried, I didn't feel like myself, and I desperately wanted to in a world where chaos had erupted. My weight and maintaining what I had was a concern for my oncologist, but I decided I wasn't going to force myself to up my protein intake or force myself to eat when I didn't feel like it. My taste buds would change, and my appetite would waver, and I went with the flow. What I did give into, though, was cravings. Whatever I wanted to eat, I ate, without thinking about the consequences my postcancer body would face.

When it came time for me to face those consequences, I was wildly unprepared. Prior to becoming sick, or rather, before I knew I was sick, I felt like I was in a good place with fitness. During the first lockdown during COVID, I began doing at-home workouts, and my body transformed. For the first time in my life, I felt strong. I could see and feel the results. That all went away.

Now it has been about four months since my last treatment and two months in remission, and my body has transformed again, but not in a way that I like. I've gained back the weight I lost and then some. I no longer fit into most of my pants. Currently, there are only two pair of jeans that still fit me. When I look into the mirror in the morning, getting dressed for work, I see my stomach sticking out in ways it has not before. Prior to becoming ill, I had been between sizes two and four. Now, I'm a size six. Realistically, a size six isn't big by any means, but it's the biggest I have ever been. The struggle I have faced to find jeans that fit comfortably and still look good on me was something I wasn't prepared for. It's a defeating feeling that makes me want to disappear.

In that same reflection, I see someone who has hair coming back. It's short, but it's back. This is a small victory, a welcome into the life without cancer. Yet I don't know what to do with it. I can't wear headbands or headscarves unless they also cover a small portion of the tops of my ears because with the full ear showing, I feel like Dumbo. I feel it and worry that it isn't coming back as strong in certain areas of my head, so I worry that others notice, and it feels like a target is on the back of my head.

I'm using shampoo, conditioner, and taking supplements to help it grow faster, as fast as it can. I'm craving hair that I can play with and style, unlike what sits atop my head currently. Sure, I'm lucky to have hair growing back, but the pixie look I have now made me feel masculine, especially on days I don't wear makeup and want to wear a baseball hat. Again, my femininity has been stripped, and I'm left feeling exposed in ways that make me want to hide from my closest friends, family, and the world. After all I've been through, you might think I want to go and celebrate my achievements, but that's the last thing I want to do. I don't like what I see when I look at myself, so how could others like me?

This plays into the bone-chilling loneliness I feel, because how could anyone understand? How can I tell the people who love me most that I don't love myself? The stage I find myself in now is what is known as liminal. To be liminal means to be disorientated because a person—in my case, myself —isn't who he or she once was and still has not become someone entirely new and solid.[5] I'm not who I once was, and even though I'm someone new, I'm not solid. I'm still swaying in the storm, but I'm slowly making my way out and discovering who I don't want to be in my post-cancerous life. I'm not sure who she is yet.

# Ready to Quit

My world was rocked, and the hits kept on coming. Bombs were dropped left and right, and I was left to deal with the aftermath. I know I could have gone to various support groups, but the idea of sitting in a room, whether it was in person or virtually, talking about how I was sick and what I was feeling felt foreign to me and not the least bit productive. I felt that talking about what was going on wasn't going to change anything, so I didn't want to do it. I also wasn't keen on talking with the people who knew me best about what I was truly and deeply feeling, let alone strangers who were experiencing the same thing, which should have been a time of bonding and a break from my isolation. I wanted nothing to do with it.

This isn't to say I didn't talk to anyone. Eventually, it came time when I was ready to talk to someone, and it was my longtime therapist. I've been going to therapy since I was fourteen years old to deal with the deaths in my family that I had experienced as a child. At first, I went through my school district, and that was short lived. A few years went by, and I had met Renee, whom I have been seeing for a decade. I decided it was time to talk because

I had reached a point in my journey where I was absolutely set on no longer wanting to continue treating my cancer.

There comes a time in everyone's lives, whether they are healthy or not, that they come to a breaking point. I went from going to the doctor when needed or yearly for a check-up to a huge fluctuation of hospital visits and then back-to-back appointments for imaging, biopsies, and other various tests to determine what kind of cancer I had. Upon diagnosis, it slowed down a bit to every other week, but it was still frequent. My life now revolved around when I was going to the doctor and how long I would be there, which, chances were, at least an hour, if not more. I was constantly being poked and prodded, getting blood drawn, having chemotherapy run through my veins via my port and then my post chemotherapy immune boosting shot. A Neulasta Onpro was placed on my stomach, and twenty-seven hours after treatment, the medication would begin to enter and be delivered in about thirty minutes. That doesn't sound too bad, does it? Sitting in a comfortable recliner for three hours every other week, with your own personal television, snacks, and drinks offered as needed. I didn't mind the chemotherapy portion per se because I got to relax for three hours and focus on myself. It was the postchemo portion that I came to quickly dread.

I was hopped up on anti-nausea meds and steroids to counteract the various side effects of the four chemotherapy drugs I was on. The steroids kept me up at night and were specifically prescribed to help with the joint pain I would inevitably experience. I was lucky enough to not have the cancer affect my bone marrow, but because I'm young, and my bone marrow was so active, the chemotherapy attacked it just as hard as it did the cancer. The chemotherapy didn't care what cells were what—if they multiplied quickly, they were being surrounded to be reduced to nothing. To say it sucked would not even come close. I had never been in such excruciating pain in my life. It was late in July, only two treatments done, and I wanted to quit. That's right, quit. I no longer wanted to continue treatment. I was set on having the stage 4 cancer that was from my neck to my groin take over my entire body. I was adamant, told my mom I wasn't going back for more chemotherapy, and nothing would change my mind. I was telling my mom that I was ready to die, no words a parent ever wants to hear from his or her child, no matter the parent's age.

I was stubborn before I got sick and even more so now because I learned no one knows what's better for me than me. I had to advocate for myself to even discover I had cancer, and I wasn't going to give that advocating up now. No one could ever be able to fully understand the deep pain I was feeling in the lower half of my body, plus my jaw, so they couldn't make any decision for me. Even if I wanted to explain what the pain felt like, I would not be able to find the words, and there was no way for me to come out about it forthright. The tears came when I was alone and able to be fully vulnerable without showing it to others because I didn't want anyone to worry about me any more than I knew they already were, especially since I'd issued this ultimatum.

I couldn't move; I couldn't find relief. The joints in my legs, knees, and ankles ached. My young and active bone marrow was being attacked by the chemotherapy, and my legs would cramp up, sending pain throughout my body. I couldn't stretch the pain away, lying in bed was a struggle, let alone getting out of it. I'd never had a feeling like this before. I would have done anything to feel relief, and I tried a lot of different methods to make the pain stop. Ibuprofen, Tylenol, ice, heat, warm baths, and nothing worked. I was prescribed an opioid for the pain, and it worked, slightly, but for obvious reasons, I didn't want to take it if I absolutely didn't have to, especially when the pain returned only hours later. This pain made work and sleep difficult and my life, which was already exhausting, that much more difficult. Strangely enough, lying on the hard floor seemed to bring the smallest amount of relief, and I took it, until my body couldn't manage the stiffness that resulted. I remember crying about the agonizing discomfort when I had a moment alone and no longer wanting to submit myself to this. After this I was switched from the Neulasta to a different immune-boosting drug that I would now have to give to myself; yep, I would be giving myself four shots over four days to keep my immune system from crashing.

The new drug was Zarxio, and once again, the pain returned. Over four months of treatment, every other week, I was suffering from tenderness in my legs, and I tried everything to relieve the pain. Despite it all, I persevered and completed all my treatments and most of my immune-boosting shots. After my eighth round, which would be my final round of chemotherapy, I refused to complete these shots. I should have because it was October, cold and flu season around the corner, but I wouldn't do it. I had made my decision to continue treatment up to this point to combat the disease, despite my strong desire to simply end it all, and I wasn't going to subject myself to any more pain if I didn't necessarily have to. I knew this might change if I had my blood drawn and my white blood cell count was too low and my doctors told me I had to use the medication. Then the cycle of pain would have started right back up again.

11

# Jealousy

When I became sick, I expected to be on a roller coaster of emotions, jealousy being one of them, as people in my life and those I followed online got to live their lives as if nothing had changed. The truth was that nothing had changed for them. I was the one who'd changed It wasn't easy, and the fear of missing out was difficult to manage. On the other hand, the jealousy I experienced toward one individual in a comparable situation was unexpected and unwelcome. This jealousy came about a month after my diagnosis. The ugly green-eyed monster that lurks about makes an appearance when you least expect it. You tell yourself it's nothing, to remain calm and not give into it by attempting to play it cool as if nothing was bothering you. In fact, the opposite is true. There's no playing it cool when you're jealous, and the more you tell yourself everything is okay, the less okay it seems. Admitting you're jealous isn't easy, but we all go through it at one time or another.

Initially, I was jealous of those around me in my everyday life. On the outside, their lives seemed normal and easygoing while I was still trying to adjust to my new reality. No one's life is easy, and we all fight battles we don't talk about, but I was in my own pity party, stuck feeling so sorry for myself that I couldn't help being envious of others. As soon as I was diagnosed, I realized that any traveling plans I had thought of or planned for the summer would have to be postponed indefinitely. There was no leaving or escaping to somewhere else, and I couldn't simply act as if everything were fine and completely normal.

My life would now revolve around the doctors, home, and work, where I had to be extremely careful, mask up, to not catch any illnesses floating around, such as COVID, because of my new highly compromised immune system. I was stuck and back to masking up in the dead heat of summer. Truthfully, this didn't last too long, but I did remain cautious. I was a cog in the machine living like a robot, doing the same thing day in and day out, living life on autopilot. Waking up, going to work, eating lunch, back to work, driving home at the end of the day. That is it. This pattern would repeat itself five days a week. The only differentiation in my schedule would be doctors' appointments and the occasional get-together with friends at my house outside. Normally, a consistent schedule is something I crave. I'm not a huge fan of surprises or change. I like dependability, routine, and structure. Control over my body and life is what I crave, and at that point, I had none. I couldn't necessarily control what was happening internally, and this led to an imbalance externally. The repetition in my days, which I had once dreamed of, bored me and made me feel like I wasn't remaining intact but rather spinning out of control with no tangible way to settle down. The plans I had made became disrupted, and as much as I was spinning, I was simultaneously stuck.

I couldn't go on vacation, take a day trip, or go to a concert. That is what summer was for, and all the plans I had suddenly disappeared in a puff of smoke right in front of my eyes. Even plans I was attempting to make months away seemed impossible.

Everywhere I looked, it was as though other people were living life like I used to have and desperately still wanted. I was bombarded with photos of beaches, concert updates, and an ever-revolving door of listening to people making plans to do anything and everything. No matter how good I felt or yearned to go, I knew deep down I couldn't go even if I took all the necessary precautions. Under no condition would my mom or sister let me leave the house except for work or when I was going to the doctor. I couldn't do a thing about it. Jealousy slid right into my everyday life like it was a piece of the puzzle that was somehow missing now coming into place.

The jealousy that came later, which I didn't expect, was when a former high school friend of mine shared his diagnosis with stage 4 cancer. It was August 4, just over a month after my own diagnosis, I had just completed my second treatment. It was late at night; I couldn't sleep from the prechemotherapy steroid given to me. I was scrolling through social media and came across a GoFundMe for a former friend and high school classmate, Connor. Connor had also recently been diagnosed with cancer. His was also stage 4, but it was colon cancer. I was beyond devastated. I knew all too well what he was going through and was heartbroken. He didn't deserve to be sick. Simply knowing he would be going through some similar situations was one of the worst feelings I had ever felt. I never wanted anyone to feel how I felt or to go through this at such an early age.

Normally, I would have been asleep for hours, but I couldn't sleep, not now, not with this information. I reached out and shared my own diagnosis with him. Our friendship was reignited. He was the only person in the world who had known what it was like to be our age, healthy, and suddenly fall ill in one of the worst ways possible. He understood what I was going through. As much as I was grief-stricken for him, I also felt relief knowing I wasn't alone and that it wasn't a stranger to whom I was talking. I didn't know how much weight had been resting on my chest until I started speaking to Connor. I had so much information, thoughts, and feelings I wanted to pour out to him because, finally, someone else understood. They would be facing similar challenges and have the same questions as I, even some of the same side effects. Connor made something that was almost unbearable bearable.

I knew my type of cancer was highly treatable. On the other hand, colon cancer was not. In his case, he had more than one area that chemo needed to shrink before he could have the surgery he would need. I only needed chemo and radiation, no surgery necessary besides the placement and eventual removal of my port. He was also away from home and his parents, living in Boston with his girlfriend. I give him huge credit for this. I couldn't imagine being away from home throughout this. My mom and sister became my caretakers, and without them, I wouldn't have made it out in one piece.

One would expect I'd be relieved that my cancer seemed to be easier in comparison. While I was, I was also jealous. It sounds ridiculous, to be jealous of someone who is in a worse situation. See, I wasn't jealous of him necessarily, but of what it seemed like he had that I didn't. The people in his corner up in Boston set up a GoFundMe for him, which is how I found out he was sick. Once the initial shock wore off, I watched the money raised to help him through this increase day by day. I was over the moon for him, because if anyone deserved it was him, but burning within me was extreme jealousy. As much as I wanted to stop checking on his GoFundMe, I couldn't stop. It was a secret obsession I had, and I felt compelled to look multiple times a day.

Alongside the jealousy was anger. I was disappointed in myself for feeling jealous of the only other person who knew what I was going through. The feelings of guilt and shame came too. It was extremely embarrassing that I was jealous of the money Connor was earning to save his life. The anger not only stemmed from the disappointment I was feeling in myself, but also at those closest to me for not setting up a similar GoFundMe for me. To which my sister responded that because of patient financial assistance I received through the network of providers and doctors I had seen for years meant I didn't have to pay out of pocket for any doctor's appointments or chemotherapy. Through this program, I had 100 percent coverage for visits and such. I used my insurance for prescriptions, which made the out-of-pocket costs for me little, a dollar at most for certain prescriptions.

Financially, I was better off than Connor was. I didn't have to pay rent or for my treatment. Yet I was still working as much as I could because other bills in my life needed to be paid, and I didn't want to fall behind and rely on the money I already had saved in the bank. I've had an unhealthy relationship with money for years. Growing up, I'd seen my parents struggle and fight about money, which made me hyperaware of how much I was bringing in with each paycheck and the amount going out for my car, insurance, student loans, cell phone, and subscriptions. I had manifested in my mind that I needed to save as much money as possible to be able to move out one day and do the things I wanted to do. While this was true, I developed an unhealthy relationship with money to the point where I would go out shopping and buy clothes, only go back to the store the next day, and return items I had bought because I was paranoid that I'd spent too much of my own money. This is why I worked throughout my treatment. I knew, if I went on disability, I would only be granted a portion of what I made and I would not be able to handle that when most days I could work through what was going on with my body. I was also lucky to have sick time to use, so on days when it seemed nearly impossible to work, I could use some of that time to get back on my feet for the days to follow.

I was deeply hurt when my sister told me I didn't need the GoFundMe because of my ability to work and have my treatments taken care of. She didn't understand the stress I felt about going to work, not because I necessarily wanted to go, but because I felt like, financially, I had to or it would ruin me. Going on disability would not have financially ruined me, but in that moment, I couldn't think straight. I was blindsided by the fortune of someone else sick like me. I told my sister that it wasn't about the money, even though it was. I wasn't worried about the cost of treatment but rather what I could have done with any extra money that had come my way. I was still reeling about the situation with my first wig and knowing I'd spent hundreds of dollars of my own money on something I didn't like at the time, couldn't return, and wouldn't get reimbursed for. I thought, if I had even a fraction of the money that had been donated to Connor, then I would not have to go to work. I thought I could take the time off that my body and mind needed to focus on healing no matter how much going gave me something to do so I wasn't stuck at home in my own bubble with my thoughts running rampant and not in a safe way.

This is easily the worst I have ever emotionally felt. It was hard to fathom that I was angry over someone else getting the help they needed. I was getting what I needed from those in my life through support, food, help at work, and so on, so I should have been glad he was getting the help he needed. I never told Connor I was jealous; I couldn't admit that to him. So, Connor, if you're reading this now, I'm sorry. When the guilt and shame came to the forefront, I began to talk to my longtime therapist, Renee. It was at this point that I knew I needed to talk to someone outside of my life, outside of what was going on, who was going to tell me like it was, and I could accept the hard truth from her. I closed out of his GoFundMe and never looked back. Eventually, a benefit was thrown for me, and I got some money that helped ease my nerves. I was able to use that money to help me write this book. To everyone who helped get the benefit together, thank you. You did more for me than you'll ever know.

At this point, the jealousy I felt turned into something different and better. The negative emotions and feelings that had grown over the past few weeks transformed into positive energy that would heal rather than hurt. I was able to take all the information I had learned since my diagnosis and put it to beneficial use by sharing the wealth of it with Connor. I was able to share the chemotherapy drugs I was on, the side effects I had been experiencing, and a little of what I simply picked up along the way. For example, ask your oncologist for a numbing cream and glop it on top of your port and cover it with a little bit of plastic wrap an hour or so prior to chemotherapy. This numbed the area and made an enormous difference when the nurse put in the needle used to deliver the medication. Another tip you might not think of was to create a binder with various tabs. I kept all the paperwork the nurses gave me about the various chemotherapy drugs and their side effects, information about prepping for a PET scan, any letters my insurance company sent in the mail, and so forth. This way I had all the valuable information organized and at my fingertips.

12

# Wishing to Be Sick

S ummer was over, and the pain from my postchemotherapy treatment was dwindling. I had gone through one initial PET scan to determine what stage the cancer was and four biweekly rounds of chemotherapy, which equated to two complete cycles. There was a total of eight weeks of treatment that had been done thus far. I was gearing up for my next PET scan. I was nervous about what this scan would show. Was the chemotherapy working, was I making the right kind of progress, would changes have to be made to my treatment plan, and how many more rounds of chemotherapy would I need? These were only a few of the questions that were bopping around in my head.

If you've never had a PET scan, consider yourself lucky. For this type of imaging to be completed, a small amount of radioactive sugar called fluorodeoxyglucose-18, or FDG-18, for short, is injected into your bloodstream via an IV. The FDG-18 is a tracer that will go where the cancer is in your body and glow because cancerous cells have a higher metabolic rate than normal cells. Thus, doctors can determine if, where, and how much cancer there is in a specific portion of your body. A special diet needs to be followed for a full twenty-four hours prior to the scan; you're supposed to limit the amount of carbs you eat and avoid sugar. Inaccurate results can occur if you don't follow what they call a high-protein/low-carb diet because the scan is looking for signs of high glucose consumption by cells This was an enormous struggle for me because I have a huge, sweet tooth and love to eat carbs. I normally didn't think too much about what I was eating, because I'd never had to before. I was encouraged to eat a diet high in protein, which was very much not me. Sure, protein was part of my diet, but nowhere near enough for it to be considered high in protein, so rather than force myself to eat in a way that felt abnormal, I ate a lot of vegetables, and incorporated protein when I needed to. Truth be told, I did cheat and have a small portion of pasta once.

Initially, my oncologist thought that I would begin with eight rounds, or four cycles, of chemotherapy spanning sixteen weeks. I was now at the halfway point of treatment, and this PET scan was ordered to see how I was progressing on my current treatment plan, ensuring the chemotherapy drugs Adcetris, Velban, Doxorubicin, and Dacarbazine were working according to my oncologist's plans. I wasn't worried about the scan itself—it was easy: get the radioactive sugar injected, wait an hour in a dark room in a recliner under a warm blanket, and then lay in a tube while it did what needed to be done, taking images of my body from my head to groin. When it was completed, I was free to go and resume a normal diet. Drinking a lot of fluids was encouraged to flush the minimal amount of radioactivity out of my body. On the other hand, I was anxious about the results; those I would not receive for a few days until I saw my oncologist again to go over the radiologist's findings.

I felt decent; therefore, I thought the treatment was working, but to what extent I wasn't sure. I was lucky to not be experiencing some of the harsher side effects, such as neuropathy, diarrhea, fever, rash, metallic taste, constipation, or vomiting. I mostly felt some fatigue and joint pain, which as we know wasn't a direct result of the chemo itself. I was getting more energy back, more than I'd had in months, but still not what I'd had precancer. In the months leading up to my diagnosis, I had been weak and tired all the time no matter how much sleep I got. Things were changing, moving in the right direction. At this point, I hadn't seen the images from my initial PET scan, which bothered me. I wanted to see the cancer to really understand the disease and what it was doing to me.

My initial scan was done at the end of June 2022, and when the radiologist's written findings were complete, they made their way to my patient portal without a doctor calling to give the results. I did what anyone else in my situation would do, my own deep dive. With Google by my side, I broke down the doctoral jargon and determined where the cancer was in my body, which was my armpits, chest, middle lobe of my right lung, and groin. My spleen was also slightly enlarged. This was why there had been a buildup of fluid around my heart and in my right lung. Determining this information on my own wasn't ideal, but I wanted answers, and this was the way I was going to get them after the regular business hours at the doctor's office.

Even though I was armed with all that information, I was still unable to place myself on a stage scale. Without the images, I was unable to truly see where the tumors were and just how much of my body had been taken over by this disease. Reading about it and physically seeing it were two different things. I couldn't determine how large the tumors were—was it just one large tumor or many smaller ones positioned together? I didn't know. Deep down, I knew the outcome from my first scan wasn't good, but I wasn't ready to fully admit just how bad it was. Somewhere in my brain, I knew it was stage 4, and I was right. I assumed it to be stage 4 because it was in multiple areas of my body, but in fact, it wasn't because it was throughout my body. Rather, it had moved from my lymphatic system to my right lung. Neck, chest, armpit, groin, and even the spleen are all part of our lymphatic system, so once it spread throughout its entirety there, it went to the next closest organ, my lung, specifically, the lung where I'd previously had pneumonia back in February.

After my second scan had been completed, I asked if there was a way for me to have a copy of not only this scan but also my initial scan so I could do my own comparison and finally see the cancer for myself. Nancy Drew was on the case and ready to solve the mystery of what was going on with my cancer. The doctor who performed both my scans had told me after the second scan that things looked good. Good? What did that mean exactly? Good as in the treatment was working or good as in the cancer was gone? My mind was racing. Once I was home, I wasted no time inserting the disk with both scans into my computer to bring them up, so I could see it with my own two eyes to grasp what was being considered good. The initial scan loaded, and goose bumps immediately formed. It was hard to believe that I was seeing my body and how much it lit up with the cancer running through my body. Reading and deciphering the technicality of it was one thing, and it desensitized it in a sense. Reading versus seeing are two completely different things. Seeing is believing, but I couldn't believe what I saw.

Nothing could have ever prepared me for what the first scan showed. Knowing the cancer was everywhere it could be, and seeing it are extremely different. It was more abstract before I saw the images. My scan was completed in black and white. Cells that had a high metabolic rate and a high consumption of sugar appeared as notably dark or black spots. The amount of black that appeared on the images, aka the tumors illuminated by the radioactive sugar tracer, appeared to me as being quite literally everywhere. It looked to me as if my body had been taken over by something foreign. Except it wasn't foreign, but rather my own body attacking itself.

Again, I thought how unbelievable it was that the cancer was able to spread the way it had without being caught sooner. The anger returned, I was completely overwhelmed with emotion and pure horror. My entire body went numb. My own body was attacking itself, and the proof was right in front of me. My mind was no longer racing but rather spinning uncontrollably. Anything compared to this seemed like it could be deemed good. Next thing I knew, I was fumbling around attempting to bring up the new scan I had that day. Nothing less than pure shock came next.

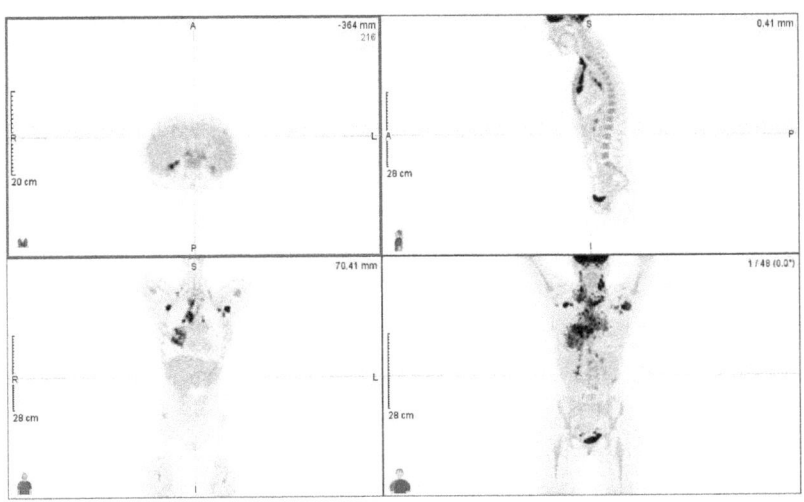

PET Scan #1 6/30/22.

I went back and forth a few times to ensure that I had mentioned the right image because the impossible seemed to have occurred. The doctor was wrong. It wasn't good; it was great, from a medical standpoint. The cancer was nearly gone. The large black splotches that had been highlighted in the first scan seemed to have disappeared. I thought I had loaded the disc in my computer wrong because I couldn't believe what I was looking at. I refused to let anyone see it because I was concerned I was misinterpreting what I was looking at or that the scan wasn't of me but someone else.

At this point, I had days to go until I saw my oncologist. The office was closed, and I wasn't sure if she was on call or not. Even if she was, I knew the doctor on call hadn't yet had a chance to look over the image and report from the radiologist, and even if she had, was she really going to go over it all with me over the phone? I had all this information, determined not to tell anyone, and was left to steep in it. To say I was going stir crazy is an understatement. You would think I would be ecstatic, determining on my own that my cancer had practically vanished after only four rounds or two complete cycles of chemo. That couldn't be further from the truth. I was petrified. The anxiety coursed through my body for days. I could barely sleep or function until the afternoon I saw my oncologist.

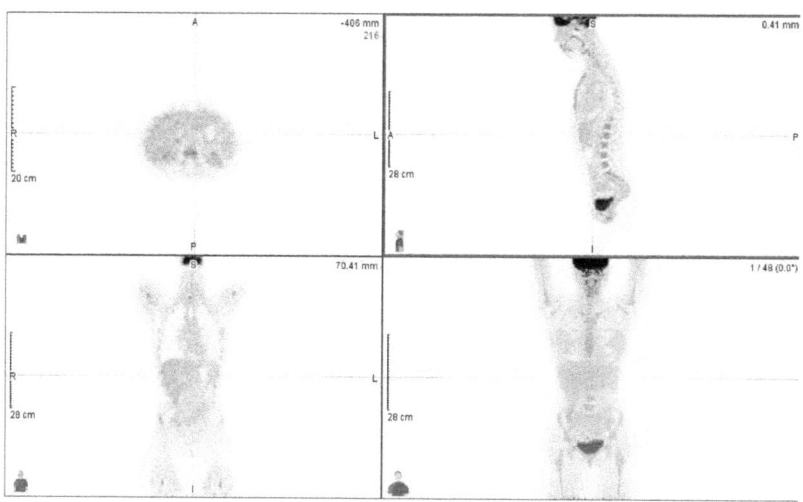

PET Scan #2 8/19/22.

I knew I should be enthusiastic that my treatment was working, but I wasn't ready to be cancer free. Internally, I was hoping I could be sick for a little while longer; it was as if I had just begun to wrap my head around being sick and what it meant for my life. To then be considered healthy again so quickly didn't sit right with me. Not enough time had passed in my mind to go from the worst stage of cancer there could be to almost nothing. How could that even be possible yet the reality I was facing? I knew no one would be able to understand my thought process here, specifically since I wasn't fully considering a swift recovery as the best news. If I had told anyone that, they would have thought I was crazy. I began to think, if this is it, then I wished I hadn't shaved my head. I kept racking my brain thinking of ways I could have changed or done things differently.

In truth, I knew everything I had done up until this point was what I needed to do at the time to get through what was happening. Part of me didn't want to get better just yet. I wasn't ready to accept any new fate and move on with my life. Unfortunately, that's not how life works. It just keeps on moving even if we aren't ready for it. The results were in, and I kept whispering to myself, "Please let me still be sick," over and over until it became a plea of sorts. I was practically begging for another chance at being sick, not really considering it would mean more chemotherapy, which would inevitably lead to more pain from the immune-boosting drugs. Twisted, I know.

Most of the cancer had shrunk or was completely gone in certain areas of my body. My spleen was back to normal size, and the cancer was gone from my groin and armpits. However, there were still tumors in my chest and right lung. This meant anther four rounds, or two cycles, of chemo over another eight weeks. When my oncologist said this, I felt a sense of satisfaction and relief. I was content with still being sick.

While part of me was relieved by this information, the other part was scared. I should have been over the moon, but I felt like every part of me was being jostled around, especially my thoughts.

Before I had gotten fully adjusted to my life with cancer, I was almost pushed into a new life without it. I could never go back to who I was before cancer, and I wasn't ready to be someone without it so soon. I had to determine who I was going to be once I entered remission because I was there and I needed to figure it out. I desired some hint or path to follow into life without cancer. I wanted to have something to look forward to, besides simply being alive, which in theory should have been enough for me to want to continue to fight and make it to the other side. I had no clue who I was going to be once everything was all said and done, which frightened me. I couldn't simply fall back into the place I was before I had gotten sick. I would not fit there anymore. My life was on one trajectory before cancer, and now I was in a completely different place and body without the faintest idea of what to do when I got better.

Before I was sick, I was in the middle of interviewing for a teaching position in the school district of Norwich, located in upstate New York about an hour away from my hometown. I had been through the initial interview at the beginning of June when I was first admitted to the hospital. This is when the doctors thought I might have an autoimmune disease. Lucky for me, I had impressed those at Norwich enough to make it to the next stage in the interview process. This meant that I would prepare a lesson and teach it to a group of students while being observed. I have been observed teaching lessons before, as part of my master's program, specifically throughout my time student teaching and in the interview process for another school district.

No matter how many times I have created my own engaging lesson and subsequently taught it while being watched under a close eye, it is just as nerve-racking as it was the first time. You never know what will happen with a group of students, especially ones who don't know you, and you never know if those observing you will like what they see. Since I was still in the hospital, I had to postpone this demo lesson and then later completely pull my application because I didn't know when I would be feeling better again. The best-case scenario for me would have been to make it through all the interview rounds and offered a position, but something in my gut told me if that happened and I later had to resign, I would have felt guilty for taking up so much of their time to only leave them in the same position as when they'd started, now with less time to find someone to fill the position. At the time, I had no concrete answers to what was going on with me, and I knew something was wrong, but no one could quite figure it out. Norwich was completely kind and understanding when I pulled my application after having to postpone my observation, but it nonetheless made it heartbreaking.

Truth of the matter was I didn't want to pull my application, and I felt like I had a great shot at getting a job offer, but I needed to withdraw myself until I had a handle on the discoveries made at the hospital that weekend. In the blink of an eye, everything I had ever worked toward in my life for at least the past three years had been taken away from me. Sure, nothing was official at this point, but I knew I wouldn't be able to move an hour away from home and start the next phase of my life if the worst-case scenario happened, and it did.

Hopelessness started to creep in, and I knew I would have to spend at least one more year living at home with my parents working at the same job I had been at for seven years already, just in a new position with a new title. I simultaneously began to live in the past and yearn for the future that had been stripped away from me. I couldn't fully let go of the dream in my head and plans I had made in my own imagination. At the same time, I didn't want to move forward with the cards I had been dealt. Despite it all, I knew how dangerous it would be if I let my mind wander and stay in the past forever because it would inevitably drag me down when I had much bigger things to worry about.

# 13

# Depression and Anxiety

Depression is a sadness, gloom, or a condition of general emotional dejections and withdrawal.[6] Meanwhile anxiety is distress or uneasiness of mind caused by fear of danger or misfortune; a state of apprehension and psychic tension.[7] When you put both depression and anxiety together, you get me. I first noticed anxiety taking hold of my life in 2013 when I was in my third year of high school. I was sixteen years old. During this period, my best friend's mom had been diagnosed with and killed by cancer, mirroring a point in my childhood when my own mother's best friend had also died of cancer. The death of my friend's mom took me back to my childhood, and it felt like I was eight years old again with another important female figure and motherly influence in my life vanishing before my eyes. This time, it was almost worse because I was older and didn't know how to console my friend who had just lost her mother. It was something I couldn't fathom even though my own mother had battled cancer just two years prior.

My panic attacks were happening at home instead of school, which made it easier in a sense because I wasn't thinking about friends or peers viewing me in that state. I would wake up and feel paralyzed. My entire body was stiff. I would be hunched over, curled into a ball because I felt that if I straightened up, I would fall apart. I wasn't in pain, but I was doubled over clutching my stomach. I had never experienced something like this before; I couldn't feel anything yet, I felt everything at once. I was sad. I was hurt. I was overwhelmed. I was in a deep state of grieving. For the first time, I became hyperaware of my heartbeat and felt overstimulated by it all. I vividly remember being curled over just trying to walk from my bedroom to the couch in the living room and believing it was an impossible feat. Most days I couldn't make it through a full day of school. I would become distressed and call my mom, who would pick me up during lunch. I would be home for the rest of the day. In some ways, it's a miracle I passed all my classes that year, considering I missed my fair share of them.

The two ways I dealt with my newfound anxiety were puzzles and therapy. Puzzles were a great distraction; they allowed my brain to think about anything else besides my grief. My hands felt like the only body part I could freely and comfortably move when I was having a panic attack. Puzzles kept my body moving and allowed me to slowly relax and loosen up.

To say my parents were concerned was an understatement. They knew something was wrong, but didn't know the full scope, nor did they know how to help me. It came to a point where my parents had seen me have multiple panic attacks, loss of appetite, and a significant weight loss to enroll me in therapy. This wasn't the first time I had been in therapy. Two years prior, I had seen a counselor through my school district. I wasn't extremely fond of her. She was nice enough, but reflecting on the time I saw her, I began to realize she didn't know what to do to help me process the trauma I had been through as a child. Despite this, the school counselor gave me one piece of advice that has stuck with me—to write letters to those important people in my life that had passed away.

It was the first time that I had ever used writing as a form of therapy to get things off my chest, and it felt good. At first, it felt strange to write a letter to a dead person. I was never sure if I was supposed to go to their grave and read it to them or not. It was my belief that those who have passed away remain near us, watching over us. If they were doing that technically, couldn't they see everything that was happening in my life? Why did I have to write it down for them? Once I got over this mental block, I was able to freely write about what was troubling me in my life, which helped me curb what would later be diagnosed as my anxiety. Yet, when I entered therapy for a second time, I knew writing about it wouldn't work. Putting what I had been through and what I was feeling into words would be much too difficult. I was also afraid of someone finding out what I had written. What I was going through during this time felt very private, and I was extremely protective of it.

When it came to talking about my emotions as a child, I found it challenging to express my emotions in a way that came out as I meant them to. I never truly felt understood. During my childhood, there had never been anyone who legitimately accepted the grief I was going through when in such a short span of time I experienced three profound losses. I was angry at the world and couldn't grasp the fact that they were really gone. I started to question my faith but remained silent about it for years. This trauma built up, and after being buried for so long, it was reawakened in the fall of 2013. The unprocessed trauma had been lingering for years, but it finally hit me hard when I first met Renee. Renee has been my therapist for a decade now. And it's safe to say she saved my life. Renee was one of the first people that really listened to me and my side of the story without judgment. She helped me overcome feelings of loss, loneliness, despair, anger, guilt, and shame.

Fast-forward four years, and at the age of twenty, I was officially diagnosed by a doctor with anxiety and depression. I was prescribed Escitalopram, an SSRI, to help manage my anxiety/depression and have been taking it ever since. This medication has been instrumental in getting my anxiety under control. Prior to taking it, I never noticed how anxious I was or how the anxiety made me feel mentally and physically. Once I began taking Escitalopram and it had time to build up in my system, I just felt better. I felt more settled, at peace, and overall relaxed. I hadn't realized the amount of tension my body had been holding beforehand. I was sleeping better, which made it easier to focus and enjoy my life. Once I had been on this medication for about two years, I had just graduated college and a lot of changes were occurring in my life. I was unknowingly attempting to soothe deeper emotions, unrecognizable emotions with alcohol. Instead of helping, alcohol only worsened my anxiety and depression.

It was one of the most harmful and dark times in my life. I was going out too much; looking back, it felt like I was going out every weekend, much more than I had during my undergraduate years. I thought drinking would help me to escape the pain I was in, because it changed my mood. I became more outgoing. I spoke more, laughed more, danced while I was out, and felt as if nothing else mattered. I was on top of the world. Instead, the alcohol made the hurt I was running from much worse. Looking back, I had been extremely hurt, still grieving, and I hadn't wanted to face life head on. I'd had no future career plans, was back living at home, and just felt out of place and very much alone, even though so many people surrounded me I thought were my friends. Turns out, they weren't real friends, and my gut intuition was attempting to tell me that all along. I was searching for something that I was missing, without being able to put a finger on it. I thought alcohol would fix the problem when in fact it became the problem. I would start out on a high, feeling great, like the life of the party, only to be deflated by the end of the night or next morning when I woke up just as alone as I had been beforehand.

After a year or so of going out and drinking heavily, I became committed to not drinking. My last straw was at the end of June in 2020. The world was slowly reopening, and I was celebrating the end of the school year with coworkers. We went out, and I ended up going to a bar in downtown Binghamton. While there, I was miserable. At this point, I was tired of feeling like a balloon whose air had been let out. I decided to take a break and cut back as I had begun the second year in my master's program for my degree in education. After about a month or two, I decided I wanted to see how long I could go without drinking, which turned out to be almost an entire year. I could have not drunk for much longer, but decided I deserved to celebrate the accomplishment of graduating with my master's degree. Since then, there have only been a handful of times when I have gotten really drunk. I don't like the way I felt or acted when I drank regularly, so now, I choose not to engage with alcohol most of the time. I never want to slip back into being the girl I was when I drank too much. She and I wanted different things out of life.

Ten years have passed since I first met Renee. I was going through the most harrowing experience of my life, and the last thing I wanted to do was talk. Going to Renee to talk about how I was feeling postdiagnosis made it real because I wasn't just saying I had cancer to myself, but I was talking about it aloud to another person, and that made it irrefutable. This meant I had to confront the feelings attached to it. Only after Connor's diagnosis had I realized I needed to speak to someone about everything I was attempting to cope with on my own, and off to Renee I went. Initially, it felt good to talk about what I had gone through, what I was still going through, and what was yet to come. Additionally, I was finally able to get the feelings I was striving to hold closely and hide, off my chest, especially to someone who knew me well. I knew I would not be judged, and she wouldn't try to solve a problem that as far as I was concerned was unsolvable, but rather listened to me and validated what I had been thinking and feeling. For me, that was more than enough. She wasn't going to tell me she was sorry for me or ask if there was a way to help. She would listen and help me make sense of what I was emotionally and psychologically going through.

Anxiety was occurring, but it wasn't in the forefront in my mind. Depression was taking over center stage. I have had heartache and heartbreak before, but nothing could have ever prepared me for the tidal wave of utter sadness I would feel postdiagnosis. In a sense, I felt stuck while the world around me kept spinning by, going on while I sat at different doctors' appointments, motionless. I wanted to be somewhere else and someone else. I was isolated on my own desert island for cancer-stricken people, and it was unfathomable to me that there could be another person out there who could imagine what I was going through. As much as I was surrounded by people at work, my family at home, doctors and nurses at chemotherapy, and friends via text, I have never felt more alone.

I was losing weight from the treatment and felt absolute disgust when I looked at myself in the mirror or in the shower. My port stuck out slightly under my right collarbone, a constant reminder that I was abnormal in some way. Including my lack of hair, everything I saw in myself made me feel like an alien of sorts. I looked in the mirror and didn't see myself staring back at me, but rather a stranger.

I wasn't only a stranger in my reflection, but in my actions too. I felt everyday as if I was putting on an act in front of others to keep it together at home and work. I wanted to assure everyone that I was okay, except when I was in physical pain that couldn't be as easily hidden. Mentally, I was unwell but didn't want to mention it to anyone because I didn't want to be pitied. Despite the help I was receiving, I still felt helpless. I was surrounded by love from every part of my life, and as much as I wished it made a difference, it didn't. I couldn't stop myself from feeling stuck. When I did try, it was as if I was in boots trekking through deep mud, and every time I took a step forward, it felt as if I hadn't moved at all. I couldn't see any of the progress I had been making. I attempted to stick to a routine as best I could because the unknown made my anxiety worse. The unknown was a scary place, and it seemed as if I was constantly in the middle of it. There was a war happening between healthy and unhealthy cells, between my body and my mind.

I desperately wanted out of my body and out of my life. I wanted to die. In fact, I would go to bed at night hoping, sometimes begging to the void, to not let me wake up in the morning. When I would inevitably wake up, I would carry on as if no wish had been made, as if nothing happened, because nothing did. No other type of loss or ordeal hit me like this before, but how could it? Everything that occurred in my life prior happened *to* me, but not in such a proximity to who I fundamentally am. At this point, the little hair I had left from my initial head shaving was shedding. I had no new growth of body hair including my eyebrows and eyelashes. I hadn't realized I was losing hair in those places until chemotherapy stopped, and they began to grow back. My period had also disappeared for months. As much as I enjoyed not feeling the need to shave my legs during the summer and no longer deal with the pain and inconvenience of a period, I still longed for that sense of normalcy and regularity in my life. Two things in a way that made me feel like a woman.

The deep depression I was in at this time in my life was unlike anything I had ever experienced before; I was deep in a funk and wanted to be swallowed up whole. I was in pure misery. The mental agony I was experiencing was unquestionably the worst pain I had ever felt in my life. Even the post chemotherapy pain in my joints couldn't come close. Being unable to control or tame what was occurring in my mind pushed me further into the depressive state that I was already in. I remember crying out in pain when no one else was home so my family would not know just how much torment I was in. It was the release I needed. At night when falling asleep, I would silently cry, hoping my heart would stop beating. I would stop breathing because I was drained physically, mentally, and emotionally, and wanted out.

I wanted out of my body and out of this life that had been handed to me. I thought the only way out was to die and no longer to face my life. I didn't want to actively do anything to end my life. I made no plans or had ideas of actively killing myself. Truth be told, there was an instance where I declared I was going to stop chemotherapy. The postchemo joint pain I was in from the immune boosting drugs was simply not worth it. If I had to go through it repeatedly, I didn't think it was worth it to live.

These thoughts led me back to Renee because somewhere deep down, I knew I didn't want to die; I just wanted the pain and hatred I felt towards myself to diminish. I was also hit with the news that remission was possible after only four months of treatment. I was just starting to feel like I had a grip on my new life and was settling into treatment and my new body when my oncologist said

I was in the clear. This news wasn't what I expected nor what I wanted to hear. It was as if I was in a car crash and was experiencing whiplash. Things were changing rapidly, and I didn't know which way was up or down, I didn't even know what to think or how to feel. This inevitably started my understanding that I was in the process of grieving myself.

Despite the initial relief I felt when speaking with Renee, it soon wore off. All we talked about was me, which I understand is the whole point of therapy, but I was feeling such a redundancy in what I was saying because everything we discussed was my cancer and grief; they were inseparable now. I wanted more. I wanted not only to discuss what I was feeling, but also to find a solution to it. Well, maybe not a solution, because it wasn't a problem to fix, but rather a way to work through it.

Being cancer free would set up a new set of challenges that I wasn't prepared to tackle just yet. I knew I should feel elated, and if I were to truly enter remission, a weight would be lifted off not only my shoulders but also the shoulders of my friends, family, and support network. I thought, if I were to enter remission, my life would go back to normal, and I was expected to live as if nothing happened. I could never do that. I was struggling with my identity with being sick, and now I was about to have it switch again to being healthy. Luckily for me and my thoughts, another four rounds, or two cycles, of chemotherapy was ordered. After those cycles, I waited a week and then went back in for another PET scan. Any cancer that had remained in my chest area had disappeared completely. The only possibility of anything remaining was a spot on my middle lobe on my right lung. My oncologist was unsure if this was cancer or just scarring from having this lung drained of fluid twice back in June. Off to the oncology radiologist I went to. Weeks had passed, no more chemotherapy, just a second opinion my oncologist wanted. If the oncology radiologist thought my lung still had tumors, then radiation would have been applied to fully get rid of my cancer. However, no radiation was needed. On Wednesday, December 7, 2022, I was deemed in remission. The spot on my lung was simply scar tissue. I cried that afternoon when I went to the room where I had received chemotherapy and rang the bell.

Over a month has passed since the day I'd rung the bell declaring I was cancer free, and I was still grieving. In some ways, my life had gone back to normal, but what does normal even mean? My body still isn't what it was before the cancer. I have some hair growing back and have gained some weight, still don't have a period, which is slightly concerning, and my port is still in place for now. Instead of my clothes not fitting because they were too loose, I'm now experiencing pants not fitting because they're too tight. I'm not sure which way I prefer. I still see myself as a stranger in the mirror and go through my days with a smile on my face attempting to hide what I feel within. I don't think I'm that good about hiding it as I once was. I know no one truly knows the full extent of what I'm feeling unless you asked my cat, who would not be able to tell you even if she wanted to. I still have moments of extreme loneliness and hopelessness. Some days I still want to go to bed and not wake up. That is the battle I now must fight—to find who I am now.

# PART FOUR

# 2023

# 14

# A New Year

New Year's Eve has been a difficult holiday for me for several years now, this year was no different except I was a different person than in years past. The past year, 2022 challenged me in ways I didn't think I would ever encounter. Here are the raw unedited words I typed out that day.

7:15 p.m.
December 31, 2022

All day while taking down the last of the Christmas decorations inside my house, vacuuming, washing counters, rearranging, I kept feeling anxious and a nagging feeling to sit down and document my feelings as the year winds down. I managed to tick off my internal to-do list and finally sit down to write. I had to really push myself to start to write, as reflecting on the past year is difficult.

For lack of a better word, this year was hard. I fought more battles and challenges than I ever imagined. I wonder if I should be proud of it, I am, but I also wish I never had to fight them. I never wanted to be sick. I wanted to get a job away from home, I wanted to move out of my parent's house and into a place of my own, I wanted more freedom at the age of twenty-six. Yet I could not, my life was stopped in its tracks to go down a different path, one that I hadn't imagined. It makes me sad because I wanted so much more for myself and now when I think about it and the steps to get there it seems almost impossible even though I beat stage 4 cancer. I'm left thinking about how my life was going to change in exciting ways when I was stopped dead in my tracks, my life paused in one way and moving forward in another.

The third song on Adele's third album, entitled *thirty*, is "My Little Love." The song ends with a voice mail Adele left one of her friends. She is sobbing and talking about how she prefers to be alone, with her own company, never feeling lonely, but was feeling lonely. This was exactly how I have been feeling recently but struggled to nail it completely. I enjoy my own company. I have always felt I was more of an introvert, and since becoming sick, this trait worsened in a way that I'm afraid may last for the rest of my life. I have become someone who can only tolerate a certain amount of time with others before my social battery ran out of fuel. Fuel is running out because of where I'm going and the people there.

This week in between Christmas and New Year, I was home alone and as relaxing as it was to have the house to myself and get things done, I think back to the struggle of when I was sick and the lonely feeling that hung over my head for months and continues to do so. When you become sick like I had, you quickly learn who your devoted friends are and the people who will be in your life through the good and inconvenient times, and as much love as I was getting from my friends, I felt alone. I know I had Connor to talk to, the one person who could relate to what I was going through at this age, but I couldn't find the words to tell him. He was going through his own treatment, and I didn't want to bombard him with the nonmedical side of mine.

This isn't the first time I have felt like this. It has happened throughout my life during times of change. This time it is different. Not all change is permanent. I was sick, and now I'm not. I still can't put into words or writing what that feels like. Yet the change in being sick has changed the trajectory of my life forever, and being in remission doesn't change that. It feels as if the life I'm living isn't my own, but of someone else and I'm watching it firsthand. Months have gone by since treatment ended, but I still feel foreign in my own body at times. I feel as if I'm still in the process of change and reinventing myself into a different version from who I was hopefully always meant to be; anxiety can do that to a person.

I want to feel alive and inspired. Often, I find that not in my day-to-day life but online and in books. I feel myself turning inward, away from reality and into fantasy. I find it relaxing and joyful while being a cause of my anxiety at the same time. I see what I wish my life to be, living in a space that is completely mine, designing it the way I want and my deepest wish, to live in England. In 2016, I studied abroad in Bath, England, and fell in love with the country. Since then, I have wanted to move to the country. The year 2023 is coming, and I feel defeated, as another year has passed and no progress has been made toward this, which I consider to be the ultimate dream or goal. I'm closer to the age of twenty-seven and am still living with my parents. A lot of time has gone by this year, it seems, more than the allotted three-hundred sixty-five days that every year has.

Scattered thoughts from the scattered mind of mine. Here is to the new year giving more than taking and taking another step toward the next phase of my life.

15

# If You Want Me to Breathe in This Wreckage

If you want me to breathe in this wreckage, I need to be alone. I need to be able to scream into the void instead of a pillow and let the anger roll off my tongue without consequence. I need to no longer stew in my anger, but let it flow. Anger. I'm angry that I got sick, I'm angry I wasn't diagnosed sooner, I'm angry that I lost my hair, I'm angry that I lost the weight to gain it back and more, and I'm angry that cancer chose me.

If you want me to breathe in this wreckage, I need to cry. I need to be free to let the tears flow and stain my cheeks, shirt, until they fall to the Earth. I need to fill an ocean with the sadness I feel within on all that was taken from me and all that was lost.

If you want me to breathe in this wreckage, I need to be free. I need to be a stranger in another city, another country, another world. I need to not be known, blend right in and experience something new, something that makes me forget who I am. I want to be so blissful that I forget all that I have been through.

Author Megan Devine, whose book *It's OK That You're Not OK* I have referred to several times throughout this book offered multiple stop-and- think moments, offering different exercises to try to help those grieving better understand what they are going through. One exercise that stood out to me was support in the wreckage. Devine suggested addressing our pain by using this prompt in being free to tell not only ourselves but also others, if we chose to, what we really crave.

Above is not only what I craved but also, still, what I hope for in the future. Writing has provided me with more relief that I knew was possible.

# Epilogue

# Accepting the Unspeakable

I began to write this book to share what I had gone through, and it turned out to be the best cathartic release I never knew I needed. Before I was officially told I had cancer I had come to know deep down it was what was plaguing me once I finally listened to my body and what it was telling me. As it stands, I'm still unable to fully accept that I'm no longer sick. In my mind I know I am and can say it aloud, but I still don't necessarily feel like or look like I'm fully healthy again. I'm in what I consider to be the healing stage before remission can truly take place for me, in a state of liminality or limbo.

I also began to write this book for others. I knew in my gut that if I were suffering the loss of myself and in this grieving process throughout my diagnosis and treatment then I knew others had gone through it before, were going through it at the same time, and would go through it in the future. If those like me were searching for some sort of answer or anyone who could relate then I assumed they produced the same results I did, I could find books about grief and losing someone, but not losing oneself to a disease like cancer.

I have been able to share stories and my perspective on situations in ways that I could never share aloud. Still, there's a certain amount of trauma that I have gone through that I will never be able to fully speak about. For months my body was fighting almost in complete silence leaving only small breadcrumbs that I ignored until my body was screaming and begging me to find answers. These answers I had to fight for because I knew something wasn't right and no doctor, I had met had an answer, only tests to tell me what I didn't have. I have attempted to put into words my thoughts and feelings throughout this tumultuous period, but still there are emotions and events that I can't quite articulate no matter how hard I try to. My body is still in fight mode, I'm fighting to physically heal completely which will not fully happen until my hair grows back. We are fighting to emotionally heal from the trauma I endured physically, socially, emotionally, and psychologically.

Remission is possible. Healing is possible, I'm working on that now. It's okay to not know when you will feel like you again, just know if you try it can happen, at least that's what I hope for. Survival mode is almost ingrained in me at this point, I want to not just survive, but live. I know it will not happen overnight no matter how desperately I wish it would. It's okay to have hard rough days and it's okay to cry about what you've been through, few if any will ever truly understand.

# Acknowledgments

Truthfully, as a reader, I have never been one to go out and seek the acknowledgment or dedication page. I've noticed them and taken a quick glance as I kept flipping the pages to get to the content of the book. If you've made it this far and are actually reading my acknowledgements, then it may seem as if I have a lot of people to thank. It takes a village to care for someone who has cancer, and I won't deny that. Yet I'm here to thank two specific people.

First, Connor. I was so devastated when I found out you had cancer. I didn't want someone who I thought of so fondly to have to go through the same pain and suffering I was enduring. At the same time, I'm happy I had someone like you to talk to and confined in during the worst time in my life. Your honesty and support has meant more to me than you will ever know. Keep the faith, you'll be in remission one day too.

Second, myself. Never in my wildest dreams did I think I would ever have cancer. Every day we see horrific things happen to people we know never thinking it can happen to us. This time, it did. I want to give myself credit for not giving up even when my mind wanted me to. I want to thank my body for absorbing the medicine and healing itself from the inside out. I thank myself for pushing myself out of my comfort zone to write a book about my deepest feelings and hardest struggles. I'm proud of my honesty and vulnerability.

Remission is possible. Surviving the grief is possible too.

# Notes

1–5 Megan Devine, *It Is OK That You Are Not OK: Meeting Culture and Loss in a Culture That Doesn't Understand* (Boulder, Colorado: Sounds True, 2017).

6    Dictionary.com. (n.d.). Depression definition & meaning. Dictionary. com. Retrieved February 27, 2023, from https://www.dictionary.com/ browse/depression.

7    Dictionary.com. (n.d.). Anxiety definition & meaning. Dictionary. com. Retrieved February 27, 2023, from https://www.dictionary.com/ browse/anxiety.